A LOST TRADITION

Women Writers of The Early Church

Patricia Wilson-Kastner
G. Ronald Kastner
Ann Millin
Rosemary Rader
Jeremiah Reedy

UNIVERSITY
PRESS OF
AMERICA

187650

ACKNOWLEDGEMENTS

During the course of the production of such an extensive work many individuals and groups of people become involved, and deserve thanks. We cannot begin to name all of them, but we would offer special tribute to librarians and staff of the University of Arizona at Tempe and of Vanderbilt University in Nashville. Dr. Holt Graham, Harriet Kruze, and Janet Weiss, of the United Theological Seminary library in New Brighton, who handled the gathering of almost all the resources for the Introduction, Proba, Egeria, and Eudokia, deserve praise overflowing and cascading down.

To Marian Hoeft and Jody Johnson of United Theological Seminary of the Twin Cities, who ably typed and saw to its final form this manuscript, we give an especially hearty cheer.

To all those friends and colleagues who encouraged us, listened to us mutter and wonder, and supported us to the completion of this work, we offer our heartfelt gratitude.

TABLE OF CONTENTS

PREFACE

In January of 1973 I was scheduled to teach a course at United Theological Seminary entitled "Women Theologians of the Christian Tradition." One of my colleagues responded, in a somewhat sceptical tone, "That's going to be a short course, isn't it?"

It was not a short course; I soon found myself wallowing in a mass of medieval materials, and discovered a fair number of modern and contemporary women theological writers. But, alas, I was able to uncover very little which came from the early church, a disappointment which was reenforced for me the following semester at United when I taught "Church Fathers, a course singularly devoid of women, except as addressees or examples. We were aware of bits of Perpetua's account of her martyrdom, and the travel diary of Egeria, but no more. Was this all early Christian women had written? Was the absence of women writers from the ranks of the early Christian writers due to the inadequacy of early Christian women or their lack of education? Did these women write, but their works perish in an insidious male plot? Or were there women writers whose works lay unexplored?

Over the next couple of years other projects filled my time, but in the course of other forays into writings of the early church both my husband and I uncovered other women writers whose extant works have been briefly examined by moderns, but have never been assimilated into our general consciousness of the "Patristic Era." We finally found that there were four women authors whose works were extant: Perpetua, Proba, Egeria, and Eudokia. Neither Proba nor Eudokia had been translated into any modern language. (Later we were to learn of Diane Hatch and Elizabeth Clark of Washington College working on Proba's Cento.) Because three of these women had written works of signifi-cant size, we decided that if we translated each of these author's writings, we would have a substantial volume. Further, it seemed to answer a call we had heard from several colleagues who teach in the area of early church and, who were seeking a suitable text which presented early women writers. Thus we determined to produce the first volume of Mothers of the Early Church. In our volume we have included complete translations of all women writers of the early church, with the exception of

Proba and Eudokia, a few writings of whom are not translated completely here.

The position of these women in the world in which Christianity developed was an ambivalent one for any woman of talent and ability. Although there was much more freedom for Roman women than for earlier Greek women, it is equally true that despite certain legal and personal liberties, there were still many restrictions on women in the Roman Empire, allowing them a public role in few places and limited circumstances.[1] Women's participation in Christianity was colored by Roman religion, which allowed women only a restricted and generally insignificant place in its structures and practice.[2] From the second century B.C.E. Roman women were reported to be attracted to foreign religions, and Christianity among them did offer women a role in the institutional structure, no matter how unsatisfactory it may appear to contemporary notions of equality. While one can debate various positions about Christianity's effect on the social standing of women in the Roman Empire, unquestionably it released previously untapped well-springs of energy among women to whom the Gospel was preached.[3] Of the writings which we possess or even know about from women in the Roman Empire after the days of Augustus, only some of the poetry of Sulplicia is extant; all the other works are by Christian women.[3a]

In perspective of their culture, these Christian women writers represent a distinct achievement, and contrast to the Roman world which nourished them and their male teachers and rulers, providing women with little sense of belonging or purpose in religious institutions. Individual introductions to each of the authors will give details about each woman and her contribution. But before examining individuals we will explore the broader question of how these women writers related to the Christian community of which they formed a part. The issue is highly complex and nuanced. Although in previous literature the attitude of early Christian writers to women has been more and less favorably evaluated,[4] there has been much less attention paid to women active in the church as their activity is reflected in literature, both as writers and as written about.[5] In order to have some idea of how the women represented in this volume fit into their context, it would thus seem appropriate here to briefly sketch something of the work of women in the church of the first five centuries, with special attention to our women authors.

When one leaves the period of the New Testament, where one finds women taking a significant leadership role in the development of the early church, even in some of the prophetic ministry of its cult, we find very little data until the third century.[6] Much of the material prior to this period is composed of exhortations to suitable fulfillment of women's duties, with praise of "many women invested with power through the grace of God, [who] have accomplished many a manly deed."[7] Clement of Rome here sounds a theme which would be articulated more absolutely by ascetical writers in the fourth century: that virtue properly pertains to men, but that through grace women are also capable of being elevated to manhood. Another tension hides in Clement's comments: an implied deprecation of woman as woman, along with a recognition that in fact they have performed worthily as Christians.

Of the structure of the postapostolic church as pertaining to women, we know very little. Pliny provides us with our first glimpse of women in the second century church when in a letter written to Trajan in 111 he mentions two women slaves he has arrested for being Christians, who are called by their fellow Christians ministrae or deaconesses.[7a] Although one must keep in mind that the terminology for various Christian offices was not fixed firmly by this period at the same time one ought not to minimize the fact that these women clearly did have a recognized function with the local church. Unfortunately, one cannot say anything more about women in the structure of the church of this period. In Ignatius' Letter to the Smyrnians we learn of virgins, recognized as a class, enrolled among the widows.[8] Both the widows and these recognized virgins were supported by the church and thus were obligated to it. Polycarp, in his Letter to the Philippians, exhorts the widows to virtue, and asserts that their duty to the church is to pray for it, and to preserve themselves from sin, for they are as God's altar.[9] Wives, the most numerous group of women, are expected to perform the duties of their state, being content with their husbands and managing the household properly and prudently.[10] Polycarp is the first to mention the responsibility of wives to educate the children "based on the fear of God."[11] In this early period the wives and the widows, who sometimes include the virgins, seem to be the only sorts of women mentioned as a group. Neither do we have records of any individual woman from this period, no writings, and little mention of women in the leadership of the churches. On the other hand, we have no indication that women did not engage in some role in the church, that they might not have been allowed some teaching and ministry roles of some sort. The documentation simply does not answer our questions. At the same time, one should note that the Apostolic Fathers, the Apologists, and Irenaeus write no fulminations against women, no strictures laying down what they may not do, no barriers to their activity in the church. Although one should not allow this silence to be played into an imagined "golden age" for women, the absence of the con-demnations of individual women and women as a class of the sort that one might find in contemporary pagan literature may very fairly be interpreted as indicating a still relatively high place for women in the Christian community. Subordinate to men as she might be, the written documentation contains no castigations of women's weakness like those of later periods, elaborate lists of her flaws, nor restrictions of her activity.

The Gnostic literature and apocryphal writings give a some-what more elaborated treatment of the theology of womanhood, with an ambivalent evaluation of the role of women. In many of the Gnostic systems, there is a male-female complementarity in the Pleroma and its emanations, and Sophia cooperates in the process of Redemption. On the other hand, the female principle, often Sophia, is the cause of the fall, and the female is passive.[12] At this point, we know little about the actual position of women as a group in gnostic communities; it would be necessary to know much more about their actual functioning in communities before concluding that their position on the whole was significantly different from women in the more orthodox communities.

In various Apocryphal writings, some Gnostic to a greater or lesser degree, we have women presented as disciples of Jesus and prophets of truth (Gospel of Mary, Pistis Sophia, Questions of Mary, the Christian Sibylline books), but at the same time some negative notions about women are articulated. The same notion of the woman becoming male by virtue which occurred in Clement is even more strongly stated in some of the Apocryphal literature.[13] A similar strong tension may be observed in the Acts of Paul and Thekla, in which Thekla is on the one hand presented as a follower of Paul who became a teacher and colleague of Paul, baptizing herself and teaching many to follow Christ. At the same time a strong encratic tendency is manifest in the insistence that Thekla is a virgin, following the most noble and truly Christian life. Already in the church of this early period a model is presented to Christian women which asserted that the woman who would become a good Christian and be a teacher in the church can do so only if she is virginal, despising marriage and the flesh.[14] At the same time, the Acts provided such a forceful image of a woman teacher that Thekla was the object of popular veneration by Christians for several centuries.[15] The many references among the church Fathers to Thekla and the attempts of several to explain away the apostleship of Thekla as a special gift for her alone would at least hint that the figure of Thekla was a positive influence on Christian women as they tried to understand their role as leaders in the church.

In the third century, although the evidence for the role of women in the church is still meager, it is somewhat more abundant than in earlier years. We have from the third as well as second century specific records of some of the women who were martyrs and confessors, positions of increasing importance in the church, further reports about widows and deaconesses, as well as the virgins, and some statements about the activities of women in some of the groups that had split off from the other Christians or been rejected by them. At the same time we have more writing of the activities of women, we also have more negative teaching from bishops, presbyters, and other ecclesiastical writers about woman's nature.

Women as well as men were revered as martyrs, and as the Acts of Perpetua and Felicity tell us, such martyrdom was a charism which lifted them out of their feeble condition as women to make them the equal of males in their struggle against the Powers of Evil. All who were martyred would be immediately before God in heaven; thus they could intercede with God directly, as Perpetua's account informs us, and within this eschatological frame could even be superior to the clergy. From the beginnings of the martyrs, cult, we know that women were venerated equally with men.[16] But at the same time, one should note that no matter how great the veneration and respect for the woman martyr, whether in the eschatologically focused North African Church, or the more established churches of Rome or Antioch, the status of the woman in the church of this world did not rise.

As a prime example we may cite the great Tertullian, redactor of the Acts of Perpetua and Felicity, who on the one hand vigorously insisted that women could be martyrs as well as men might, and were equally entitled to the rights, privileges, and

spiritual gifts of the martyr.[17]   But when he needed to
make judgments about the actual conduct of women in this
world, he gave them a considerably more circumscribed role.
In On Purity he notes the existence of the body of widows
as a distinct group in the church from which he has broken
away,[18] and also speaks frequently of virginity in both his
orthodox and Montanist period.[19]   He has virtually nothing
to say about the duties of married women except to warn them
against paganism, excesses, and the temptations of a second
marriage.[20]

The one exception to this very limited and decidedly
second-class existence is in the figure of the ecstatic
prophetess, who begins to appear in his work after he became
acquainted with Montanism.   In one work, the Exhortation to
Chastity, written between 204 and 212, while he was still
only in sympathy with the Montanists, he praised "the holy
prophetess Prisca."[21]   In Against Praxeas, probably written
about 208-210, after Tertullian had become a Montanist, he
attacks Praxeas for two evils: first, he introduced a
modalist heresy into the church of Rome, and second, he
pressured the bishop of Rome, who had given his approval to
the "prophetic gifts of Montanus, Prisca, and Maximilla," to
withdraw his letter establishing communion with the Montanist
Churches in Asia and Phrygia.[22]

His acknowledgement of the prophets gifts of Prisca and
Maximilla did not, however, change the fundamental orienta-
tion of this first great Latin Father.   Some women were given
such a high position in this last period of Tertullian's writing
out of the Montanist conviction that this was the end time,
and that the demand of God on the church was for purity of
morals and chastity.   The women prophets are the vehicles of
the Holy Spirit, to be listened to with respect, but are not
given a role in the hierarchy in Tertullian's system.   Although
Tertullian refers to the Phrygian women prophets, he does not
refer to any women active in the North African church.   Furthermore, they are necessarily virgins, for only they can be
truly pure in the sight of God.

Although Tertullian never includes women in a hierarchy
of the church, the historian Epiphanius mentions a sect
apparently related to the Montanists, who had women bishops
and presbyters, but we know nothing further of them.[23]   What

xii

does seem clear is that in the Greek and Latin churches, and even in the Montanist schism, although the value of woman as virgin and even as prophet may be affirmed, she has no place in the governing hierarchy of the earthly church and is very limited in her ministry. Her worth comes through her participation in the eschatological, transcendent order which was not of this world. There is probably some truth to the argument that the "orthodox" churches reacted against the prominence of women in the heretical groups by restricting the role of women; but it seems equally true that it scarcely seems to have occurred to many of the groups which had broken off to elevate women to a place in the formal structure of the organization. Women appear to have been confined in most of the sects to the charismatic rather than the hierarchial aspect of the church, aspects becoming increasingly separated from each other during this period.

Cyrprian, the bishop of Carthage and great admirer of Tertullian, says very little specifically about women; we possess one letter of his directed to a brother bishop advising him in the correction of virgins who were pledged to celibacy, but had been living with men without having intercourse with them.[24] While inveighing against the practice, he counsels taking them back into the church with repentance. His few other comments about women also relate to virgins, and his treatise on the dress of virgins continues a moderate version of Tertullian's comments about the modesty of demeanor and manner of those pledged to virginity.[25] His words testify to the increasing significance of the class of virgins in the Latin church, and would infer a declining importance of the widows as an ecclesiastical group.

Clement of Alexandria does not lay such stress on the goodness of women as directly related to her virginity. He does not concern himself with the ecclesiastical status of women, or of men either, but as one might expect in the head of the Catechetical School, writes about the ability of the woman as well as man to achieve perfection.[26] Clement even singles out wives as a group of Christians to whom he offers advice, speaking of marriage as a state blessed by God in which happiness might be achieved.[27] Even though Clement's view of women does not lead him to comments about their roles in religious institutions he is distinguished from his Latin confreres both for his positive view of marriage and his theological rationale for the ability of women.[28] One should note particularly that for Clement virginity is <u>not</u> an essential prerequisite for perfection for women. That notion will be at least modified in later writers, and linked with the praise of celibacy which Clement renders in other contexts.

Origen does not speak about virgins as a special group within the church, or to women within the Christian community, although we know from Eusebius that he taught women in his catechetical school, and the name of one of them, Herais, has been preserved.[29] He praised virginity highly in his works,[30] but his discussion is confined to the dimensions of personal spirituality. However, by the second half of the third century an image reoccurs in literature which will appear fully developed in the life of the church in the next century. It is woman as the Virgin-Teacher. In Methodius of Olympus' The Symposium, the image of Thekla appears again, but in a somewhat different guise than in the second century Acts of Paul and Thekla. Thekla here emerges as the acknowledged leader of a group of virgins who are dedicated to the devout life, and pursue it with learning and wit. Thekla is the teacher, who gains her leadership over the others not by her piety only, but through her learning which is acclaimed by the others, her ability to interpret Scripture, and her refutations of pagan philosophy. The virginity which Thekla espouses is freer of encratic taint than that of The Acts of Paul and Thekla; it gives one freedom and one's human completion. In this perspective it enhances the woman's personhood. The virgin may even defend the goodness of marriage without feeling the worth of her own state threatened.[31] Macrina's Life written by her brother Gregory of Nyssa in the next century, will portray the embodiment of this ideal in a community of Christian virgins.

The Didaskalia Apostolorum, a third century Syrian description and explanation of church order and practice, specifically mentions two distinct groups, the deaconesses, who are ordained to a ministry, and the virgins and widows, who are not. The deaconess is "to be honored by you in the place of the Holy Spirit," and is listed along with the bishop, deacons, and presbyters. She is to stand at the entries of the church for the women to scrutinize them and to see who is to be admitted. She has very specific duties: to minister towards women in ways that the men cannot. When un-

believers would not allow or would be scandalized by a
deacon coming to women, let the deaconess go. In the
anointing at baptism, the deaconess shall anoint the women,
except on the forehead, which the deacon shall do.[32] at
the same time, it is asserted firmly that the practice of
ordaining women priests for female dieties is a pagan custom,
and sacerdotal and teaching functions are explicitly forbidden to women on the grounds of their subordination to
men.[33] Here we find the first articulation of arguments
against the priestly ordination of women based on a need to
separate Christian from pagan practice, and a further ex-
clusion of women from teaching based on inherent inferiority,
and Jesus' omitting of women from the apostles. One might
also reasonably infer, from the strong words of opposition,
some women had been assuming teaching and priestly functions.

Virgins and widows are listed, along with the older
women, as the first to stand or sit before all the other women
in the women's section of the church.[34] Widows are not further mentioned nor defined, but the virgins are held up as
individuals who make a vow of celibacy for piety, to be holy
as the dwelling of God, Christ, and the Holy Spirit.[35] Although there is no specific denigration of marriage (the virgins are specifically warned against reproaching marriage),
the virgins are given public recognition for their vow and
precedence over married women. At this time there is no indication of communities of virgins or widows; and the office of
widows seems to have grown less important in the public life
of the church, for no such obligations as prayer for the
community are attached to it.

The fourth century additions, contained in the Constitutions of the Holy Apostles, make some liturgical clarifi-
cations of the distinctions between virgins and deaconesses.
The bishop lays his hands on the deaconesses' head, and prays
over her in words which imply a function analogous to that of
the deacon in the church. On the other hand, the Constitutions
proceed to state that virgins are not to be ordained, citing
the Didaskalia's interpretation of virginity as leisure for
piety, not for a ministry in the church.[36] At this juncture
of the church's history, the church orders are quite specific
that virginity is a charism for individual perfection, whereas the deaconess has a publicly acknowledged ministry.

The third century ecclesiastical literature, as far as
one can judge, evidences a decrease in attention to both
the married women and widows, either in advice to them or
with respect to their role in the organization of the
ecclesial community. Virginity is increasingly lauded in
Latin and Greek literature, although often with different
emphases in the two literatures, as Rosemary Ruether notes.
The Greeks often wrote of it as a way to Christian freedom
in Christ, offering women a sphere of personal responsibility in a church where the eschatological fervor which had
previously held such possibilities for women was increasingly
less central. The Latins focused much more on virginity as
an aescetical practice for the taming of impure desires, although as we shall see it did become in fact a way of
achieving freedom for women in the Latin West as well as the
Greek world.

The most significant development, which signaled a
change in direction for both East and West, was the rapid
growth of the organized communities of virgins. Palladius'
Lausiac History written about 419 or 420 is replete with
stories of organized communities of women monastics which are
treated matter of factly, as coexisting with male communities,
of equally venerable age. These communities of virgins referred
to by Palladius range from 50 to 400 in number, and reflect a
high decree of organization and the following of a communal way
of life.[37] Sometimes the women's and men's monasteries seem to
have been separate; others appear to have been forerunners of
the dual monasteries of men and women that we later find in
the West.[38] We also find a wide variety of these women aescetics
in monasteries visited, from the spontaneous, cheerful, and well
beloved Amma Talis, head of a monastery of sixty,[39] to the nun
who feigned madness for many years, living off table scraps and
regarded with contempt by the others.[40] One should also note
that although the focus of Palladius' History is on Egypt,
these communities seem to extend over Asia Minor and even into
the West.[41]

Palladius also testifies to the continuing popularity of
the aescetic life in its less organized form, individual women
aescetics gathered together in the same town where there were
many women who "practiced virginity and were remarkable women
indeed." In the town of Ancyra Palladius estimates that there
were about two thousand of these women.[42] He also lists a

number of these women by name, persons from both the Greek and the Latin church: Veneria, Photeina, Asella, and most notably the virgin Olympias, widow of Nebridius, who "instructed many women, addressed priests with reverence, paid honor to bishops, and was deemed worthy to be a confessor on behalf of truth."[43]

A smaller group is also referred to by Palladius; these are the married men and women who had later decided to live a life of aesceticism and celibacy which still remaining together (not to be confused with the subintroductae).[44] Clearly for Palladius this sort of aesceticism is much rarer, and the norm for the aescetic life is either coenobetic life or the individual life of virginity dedicated to good works and prayer.

One particular figure who is of great importance in the development in the Greek world of the organized form of monastic life is Macrina, the sister of Gregory of Nyssa. In his Life of Macrina[45] Gregory outlined the organization of a community of aescetic women by his sister. Gregory informs us that Macrina convinced her mother to live in his community, and also induces her brother Basil to combat his pride by dwelling in this monastic community for some time.[46] The effect of his living of the cenobitic life under Macrina's direction must certainly be inferred to have shaped Basil's understanding of the monastic life and his own written rule. Gregory details much about the life of this small community at Annisa, emphasizing the common life, the absolute equality of rich and poor, their work, constant prayer, and obedience to the head of the monastery, Macrina, who never puts herself above them.[47]

Gregory's attitude towards Macrina is notable for another feature besides his reporting on her development skills and ability as spiritual director of the first documented organized community of women virgins among the Greek Christians. As becomes even clearer in On the Soul and Resurrection, his dialogue which is an expansion of a part of the Life, Gregory portrayed Macrina as a woman learned in the Scriptures and capable of reasoned argument, and in very exact ways presents her as a Christian Socrates, a Virgin-Teacher, who can expound the truths of the faith out of the experience of her life and rational knowledge, not only to the other virgins, but even to her brother the bishop.[48] His theological rationale for such an opinion of a woman may be found in his works on virginity, in which he locates the image of God in the human in the soul, which is thus not bound by the body, which is male and female. In the spirit, striving for God in virginity (which Gregory insists is primarily a spiritual attitude which may be found with or without physical intactness) man and women are equal before God and in progress in virtue.[49] Thus Macrina can be not only a Virgin-Teacher in her life, but also in her discourse.

Parallel to the development in the Greek world, the Latin Christian community was also experiencing a growth of women's communities of aescetics. The development of the Roman circle directed by Jerome has been well documented, showing how growing from individual women devoted to lives of prayer, study, and physical self-denial, a number were able to establish communities in Jerusalem.[50] They were noted for their study of Scripture, and very intense aesceticism, which even Palladius reports on, specifically citing Melania and Paula as examples.[51] Jerome wrote in considerable detail about the community which Paula founded in Jerusalem. In its work and constant prayer, and cultivation of virtue, Paula's community lived an existence similar to that of Macrina's; it was, however, divided into three separate groups which lived apart but gathered for prayer, nobles, middle class, and poor. All were trained in the psalter and scripture and wore the same clothing, but the nobles were allowed each to have an attendant.[52] In this class distinction one notes a difference from the community of Macrina, but in other respects a very similar cenobitic life was emerging, marked by a cultivation of Scriptural prayer and learning among those capable.

Paula's and Melania's growing community was rooted in a secure tradition of women virgins and widows in the Latin aesceticism which animated those women. It asserted that virginity gave one freedom from fleshly desires for pursuit of union with Christ; in Jerome's analysis it was bound up with a much more negative evaluation of marriage than that which one finds in Gregory of Nyssa.[54] Ambrose's temper is much more moderate in his praise of virginity, and insistance that marriage is a good state for Christians, although inferior to virginity. Nonetheless, he shows how the ideal of virginity as an asecetic armor which would protect from

harm one completely dedicated to God had overshadowed all
other aspects of virginity for women. In his treatise on
virginity Thekla is no longer the figure of the Virgin-
Teacher; she is the virgin whose state protects her from the
wild beasts who do her homage, though no mention is made of
the teacher whose mind is free to pursue the truth of Christ.[54a]
Augustine of Hippo worked within the same framework as Jerome,
paying much more attention to the evils of the flesh.[55] One
of the characteristics of this period, in the West as well as
in the Greek East is the increasing movement of virginal life
into communal life rather than the aescetic life at home,
dedicated to prayer and the doing of good works. Increasingly, the "virgins" spoken of by ecclesiastical writers are
only those organized by the church into some sort of community life. The devout virgins of whom we have read in
prior writers are to soon be mentioned almost exclusively
within the context of religious communities.

There appear also to have been some loosely organized
communities of virgins who were not monastics, although
they were pledged to a life of prayer and virtue. Palladius
mentions some of them in both the East and the West. Egeria
writes her travel journal to a group of these women at home.
Her own extended travels would indicate that such women did
not necessarily live the restricted sort of monastic life
founded by such women as Paula and Macrina, while the focus
of Egeria's diary on Scripture and the liturgy would infer
that those were the primary concerns of her fellow religious
women. Even when Egeria writes home about monastics, she
speaks in general ways about their virtue, but never discusses their rule or organization, and spends her time
noting their learning in the Scriptures. Although we possess
no firm evidence, it seems likely that Egeria's community
with its liturgical concern is at least the ancestor of the
communities of canonesses which gave such noble service to
the church before being absorbed into women's monastic
orders.[56] We do not know how widespread such groups might
have been, or if these loosely organized groups, as distinct
from individual devout virgins, were every very popular.

The other distinct order of women ecclesiastics which
continues its development during the fourth and early fifth
century are the deaconesses. In the Latin West we have no
mention of them until the fifth century, and then only to
forbid their ordination, although by the sixth century they

are permitted.[57] In the Greek church of this period they flourished, however; Egeria mentions her good friend the deaconess Marthana, who is the leader of the men and women aescetics who live around the shrine of St. Thekla, and Palladius mentions the "deaconess Sabiniana, aunt of John, bishop of Constantinople."[58] That same John Chrysostom of Constantinople is famous for his letters to Olympias, the deaconess of the church of Constantinople even after John's exile, and with whom he exchanged comments both personal and ecclesiastical about the future of the beleagured church.[59]

Palladius also mentions an anonymous deaconess who was the head of a monastery of women,[60] Gregory refers to the deaconess Lampadion, who "directed the choir of virgins" at the monastery, and was a good friend of Macrina's.[61] Such figures would indicate that women deaconesses would usually be found connected with the churches, but might also now be found in roles of leadership in the monasteries. If there were more documentation, we might have some idea of how widespread the practice was, and what its purpose was -- for instance, was the presence of the deaconess an institutional link between the monastic community and the bishop or in monastic communities did "deaconess" become a title -- and who was responsible for the deaconess' presence in the community?

But although we have an ever growing amount of literature for the virgins living a common life, and much dealing with the deaconesses and ecclesial women, by this period there is virtually no attention paid to what must have been the largest group of Christian women, those who were married and part of families. The only literature addressed to them seems to be consoling them for the loss of their spouses, encouraging them to espouse a celibate life as soon as possible, and exhorting them to a virtuous life conceived along a monastic norm.[62] Even people like Gregory of Nyssa, who seemed to have a positive appreciation of marriage, spent little time helping women develop themselves positively within this state; the effort is almost universally one of urging women toward virginity or at least the bringing up of young virgins for the next generation.

Most often when one finds a lay woman who is not a dedicated virgin written of in theological literature in

more than a passing reference she appears as the type of
the simple faithful, who knows because of her piety what
others (men) who are more theologically learned have to
struggle to discover.[63] Nonetheless, we do find records
among the church historians of active and intelligent lay
women among the ruling classes. Socrates writes in praise
of Helena, the mother of Constantine, who was an influence
on her son, and who was responsible for the erection of many
of the marvelous shrines of Jerusalem.[64] The empress Eudokia,
author of several poems and doctrinal works, is described by
Socrates, who praises "her excellent literary taste," and
her further building in Jerusalem, though little is said of
her writings.[65] Sozomen writes of the virtue of the prin-
cess Pulcheria, who educated the emperor fittingly, trying
to nurture virtue in him, and who led her sisters in the
same sort of life as one of the "exemplary women" whom
Sozomen as a matter of course assume as the devout unmarried
women dedicated to prayer, good works, living together in a
fairly unstructured way.[66]

Of the learned women who were married and attempted a
teaching task, or were noted for virtue, we have very little
contemporary evidence. Proba is known to us because her
work was very popular for several hundred years, and has
come down to us, but of her life we know little, and we have
no certain contemporary testimony of her life and work. We
have no direct record that persons such as Proba were encouraged or acknowledged within the church. And of course
for the ordinary women of the middle and lower classes there
were no works written, nor do we have any ecclesiastical
appraisal of their lives' work.

The canons which we have from fourth and fifth century
show a church where the role of women is increasingly restricted, and almost everything said of them is negative.
Part of this impression is due to the simple reality that
most laws are passed to prevent abuse, and thus one would
be deceived if one expected to read the laws and to gain a
complete or very accurate portrait of any culture. Nonetheless, the laws and legal edifice convey something of the
values of members of that society. One can also find it
highly illuminating to note what a particular society considers to be an abuse to be abolished.

Women are forbidden to dress as men, cannot marry two

brothers, may not approach the altar, speak during the liturgy, cannot be presidents of the assembly. Men suffer no such prohibitions in the canons, though each of the canons point to different ways women had attempted to gain influence in the church and community. Women are forbidden various contacts with the clergy. Numerous canons affecting the validity of marriages were passed.[67] Interestingly, in some of the early canons (e.g., of Gangra) an attempt is made to restrict the activity of women who renounce women's dress and marriage to live the aescetic life, a phenomenon which points to women's attempts to find freedom from their "femaleness" and gain access to the more influential male monastories. The role of women in institutional religion except as aescetics was increasingly restricted, and there was little canonical encouragement to women to leave the married state. (In fact, penalties are assessed if they attempted to do so.) It might be noted that there is no comparable canon restricting leaving marriage for the aescetic life for men.

In the same canon of the Synod of Gangra (c.345) preventing women in general from being presidents of assemblies, widows are specifically prohibited. Earlier canons do not formally attempt to fix the age of widows, virgins, or deaconesses, as do some later ones, for instance in the canons of Basil (c.370) requiring the virgins to be sixteen or seventeen, and a widow sixty.[68] Although the age of the veiling of virgins was prescribed as twenty-five, the African Code (419) did not penalize any bishop who should so give her the veil while she was still a minor.[69] Aside from such legislation, and practice by various bishops, there was little formal agreement about the state of virginity, which was still reckoned as a charism and not subject to general canons by the church, which claimed no more power over it than over any other lay institution.

Deaconesses of the Paulianists who come over to the Catholics are to be rebaptized, and then regarded as lay people, although the bishop may make them deaconesses.[70] However, it is not clear from the canon if this is because of the practices of the sect, whose baptism was regarded as invalid, or because deaconesses did not receive a laying on of hands (whereas the Didaskalia asserts that Catholic practice involves the laying on of hands.) The canons of the Council of Chalcedon require that a deaconess must be forty years of age, but if "having had hands laid upon her," she then tries to marry, she and her husband shall be anathema.[71] This canon would seem to support the notion that the deaconesses were among the clergy and considered set a part for an ecclesial function. No comparable language is used during this period of any other group of women.

Sweeping conclusions are not justified on the basis of our present evidence, especially because we have no notion of how many more works lie yet undiscovered, as did Egeria's until 1884. They certainly support the contention that the activities of women in the early church were of much broader scope than the works of their male contemporaries would lead us to expect. The image presented to us in the writings about women is increasingly narrow over the centuries, beginning with a more general concern for women as wives and mothers, as well as servants of the church, and narrowing almost exclusively to the image of the monastic and deaconess. To the extent one assess this literature about women, one must accept that it is narrower, more restricted, and sometimes more warped than the true picture must have been. Somewhat more reassuringly, when we look at the documents which have been preserved, we find the last witness of a young widow and mother, grieving about her family, as well as bearing witness to and praying for the church; the teaching device as well as literary feat of a noble Roman matron; the religious poetry of a cultivated empress; and the travel diary of a Spanish member of a community of religious women who are not monastics. Although this is not a social scientist's version of a representative sample, it does give us a glimpse of women functioning in a variety of active roles, and expressing themselves in a variety of ways.

Another tension with the records of women's role in the church as recorded by the "church fathers" is that although by the fourth the idealized figure of women is the Virgin, with the lay woman left out of the picture altogether, in the writings we have lay women dominate. Only Egeria, who is perhaps best described as a "proto-canoness", is not clearly a lay person. Thus a curious tension permeates the writings about women -- the impetus is towards the monasticization of the ideal woman. However, as our women writers show, that impetus did not affect the women authors of the early church, our "church mothers." Only in the middle ages will almost all the religious writings by women

be done by women monastics or aescetics who are concerned
with the interior life. The women authors of the early
church represent different sorts of women and their works
are a response to a variety of conditions and needs within
that church.

It would be quite misleading to assert that among these
writers we have introduced a new Augustine or Basil; no one
of such influence or theological profundity appears. Nonetheless, on their own terms these writings are achievements
which can stand without apology among their contemporaries.
Most important, they fill a gap the significance of which
historians of the early church are just beginning to fully
appreciate. The early church is more than the theologians
and controversies; it encompasses lay and clergy, males
and females, some of whom wrote theology which others read,
while others lived much simpler lives. In the works of these
women we are presented with new pieces to help us construct
a fuller picture of the early church, one which includes
literate and literary women with a variety of concerns. In
such an endeavor, not only is women's heritage enriched; we
all profit.

NOTES

1. M. I. Finley, "The Silent Women of Rome," Horizon VII (Winter, 1965), 57-64; Pierre Grimal, ed. Histoire Mondiale de la Femme: Prehistoire et Antiquite (Paris: Nouvelle Libraire de France, 1965) I, 386-7, 474-479; Sara B. Pomeroy, Goddesses, Whores, Wives, and Slaves (New York: Schocken Bks., 1975), 188-189.

2. E.g. Verena Zinserling, Women in Greece and Rome (New York: Abner Schram, 1972), 73; George Tavard, Women in Christian Tradition (Notre Dame: University of Notre Dame Press, 1973), 151.

3. Grimal, 484-485; James Donaldson, Woman: Her Position and Influence in Greece and Rome, and Among the Early Christians (London: Longmans and Green and Co., 1907), 148; Pomeroy 205-226.

3a. For writings of and about women authors of antiquity see Leanna Goodwater, Women in Antiquity: An Annotated Bibliography (Metuchen, N.J.: The Scarecrow Press, Inc., 1975) 35-53.

4. Tavard, 48-121; Rosemary Radford Ruether, "Misogenism and Virginal Feminism in the Fathers of the Church," in Religion and Sexism, R. R. Ruether, ed. (New York: Simon and Schuster, 1974), 150-183.

5. Sr. Mary Lawrence McKenna, Women of the Church (New York: P. J. Kenedy, and Sons, 1967).

6. For a summary of contemporary scholarship about the issues Phyllis Bird, "Images of Woman in the Old Testament," 41-88, and Constance Parvey's "The Theology and Leadership of Women in the New Testament," 117-149, in Religion and Sexism. Phyllis Trible, God and the Rhetoric of Sexuality (Philadelphia: Fortress Press, 1978) deals with more far-ranging issues which are fundamental to the Biblical practice.

7. Clement of Rome, Letter to the Corinthians, 55. (References are to the section or chapter numbers unless otherwise stated).

7a. Letter X, 96.

8. _Smyrnians_ 13.

9. _Philippians_ 4.

10. Clement, _Letter to the Corinthians_, 11; Ignatius to Polycarp, 5.

11. _Letter to the Philippians_, 4.

12. Hans Jonas, _The Gnostic Religion_ (Boston: Beacon Press, 1963), 93, 108-111, 134, 135, 176-197; R. M. Grant _Gnosticism and Early Christianity_ (New York: Harper and Row, 1959, 1966), 76-89; Tavard, _Women in the Christian Tradition_ relates some of the Gnostic mythology to orthodox Christian thought, 70.

13. Tavard, 48.

14. "Acts of Paul and Thekla," 7.

15. "Thekla" in a _Dictionary of Christian Biography_, Smith and Wace, IV, 885-888.

16. For an introduction to the cult of the martyrs and some inscriptions indicating popular esteem and ascription of honor even to women as intermediaries, Orazio Marucchi, _Christian Epigraphy_ (Chicago: Ares Publishers, Inc., 1974), 157-181. For the right of intercession, see Eusebius, _Ecclesiastical History_, V, 18, 7. Women were also acknowledged among the ranks of the confessors, having "triumphed over their sex," (Cyprian, _The Lapsed_, 2) but their position in the organization of the earthly church was not changed.

17. _To the Martyrs_, 4.

18. _On Purity_, 13.

19. E.g., _On Prayer_, xxi-xxii; _An Exhortation to Chastity_, 13.

20. E.g., _To His Wife_.

21. Exhortation to Chastity, 10.

22. Against Praxeas, 1.

23. Tavard, 55.

24. Letter 61.

25. Treatise II, On the Dress of Virgins, 430-436.

26. Stromata IV, 19.

27. Stromata IV, 20.

28. Ruether, "Misogenism . . . " elucidates some of the differences between the Greek and the Latin Fathers' theological interpretation of women. While one might quarrel with some aspects of her interpretation, the fundamental identification of the Greeks as espousing a nonsexual monism and the Latins asserting maleness as the norm for the human seems to be useful.

29. Ecc. Hist. VI, 4.

30. E.g., Commentary on the Song of Songs, II, 5.

31. Symposium -- for the defense of marriage, Logos 2 of Theophilia; for praise of Thekla, Logos 8, preface, interlude 2 after 8; Logos 8 is Thekla's discourse; Thekla leads the hymn to virginity at the end, the epilogue contains more praise, as does Logos 11.

32. J. G. Davies, "Deacons, Deaconesses, and the Minor Orders in the Patristic Period," Journal of Ecclesi-astical History 14 (1963) 3-4. The Constitutions of the Holy Apostles contains a 4th century redaction of the 3rd century Didascalia in Bks 1-6. Specific refer-ences are II, 26, 57; III, 15.

33. Const. of the Holy Apostles, III, 9.

34. Ibid., II, 57.

35. Ibid., IV, 14.

36. Ibid., VIII, 19-20, 24.

37. Palladius, Lausiac History, 33:1, 29:1.

38. Ibid., For dual monasteries, 30; for separated 29:1, 33:1, 46:5, 59:1.

39. Ibid., 59:1.

40. Ibid., 34.

41. Ibid., Prologue, 2.

42. Ibid., 67.

43. Ibid., 41:3, 4; 56:2.

44. Ibid., 41:66. The Subintroductae were women who lived with male aesceties in "spiritual marriage." No matter how lofty the motives or even practice, the problems are obvious.

45. Critical edition in Vie de Sainte Macrine, Pierre Marval, ed. Sources Chretienne 178 (Paris: Les Editions due Cerf, 1971); Makrina Kloeppel, "Makrina die Jungere: eine altchristliche Frauengestalt" in Frauer in Bannkreis Christi (Maria-Laach: Verlag ars liturgica, 1964) 80-94; Patricia Wilson-Kastner, "Macrina: Virgin and Teacher," Andrews University Seminary Studies, to appear, 1979.

46. V.S.M., 5, 6, 7.

47. V.S.M., 11.

48. V.S.M., 16025; On the Soul and Resurrection, 430-468 NPNF 2nd, 5; PG.

49. On Virginity, 1-2; On the Making of Man, 405.

50. Anne Yarborough, "Christianization in the Fourth Century: the Example of Roman Women," Church History 45:2 (June, 1976), 149-165; J.N.D. Kelly, Jerome (New York: Harper and Row, 1975) 91-103, 273-289. Jerome wrote innumerable letters to and about these

women, e.g., letters 22-34, 37-38, 40-46, 59, 107-108, 127.

51.   Lausiac History 41, 46, 54.

52.   Jerome, 108:20-21.

53.   Lausiac History, 37:12-16; 55-57; 61.

54.   Jerome, Letter 22:18-20; 48:9-11.

54a. Ambrose, Concerning Virgins, Bk. 2, (3) 19-20.

55.   Ruether, "Misogenism . . ." 168-178; Augustine, Of Continence, 379-393; Of Holy Virginity, 417-438.

56.   Joan Morris, The Lady Was a Bishop (New York: Macmillan Co., 1973) 9-15.

57.   Canon 26 of the Council of Orange (441) forbids the ordination of deaconesses; Fortunatus reports that about 540 Radegund was ordained deaconess by Bishop Mendard (PL, 88, col. 502).

58.   Lausiac History, 41:4.

59.   He wrote seventeen letters to her (P.G. 52, 549-623). See also Sozomen's Ecclesiastical History VII, 9.

60.   Lausiac History, 70:3.

61.   V.S.M., 29, 32.

62.   E.g., Jerome, Letter 54; 78; Augustine, Of the Good of Marriage.

63.   Augustine, Confessions IX, 9.

64.   Ecclesiastical History, I, 17.

65.   Ibid., VIII, 21, 47.

66.   Ecc. Hist. IX, 1, 3.

67.   Gangra, XIII, XIV: Synod of Laodicea, XI, XLIV.

The <u>Martyrdom of Perpetua</u>: A Protest Account
of Third-Century Christianity

From the beginning of the third century C.E. there sur-
vives one of Christianity's oldest and most descriptive
accounts of the martyrdom process, the <u>Martyrdom of Perpetua</u>
(Passio Perpetuae). Though the <u>Martydom</u> is worthy of special
study for a number of reasons, the uniqueness is derived
from its nature as an early Christian account of protest.
It represents a woman's response to elements of society
which she considers restrictive to people's freedom in
thought and action. Although she is the chief protagonist
within the account, she represents both male and female
united in a common effort to retain and/or restore those
rights considered fundamental to human life.

Historical research verifies that most accounts of
Christian martyrs are fictional either wholly or in part.
Those partly fictional originated in a variety of ways, such
as official statements of an actual trial, letters, written
or verbal eye-witness reports of the event. These basic
particulars were then embellished any number of times in the
form of apologetic and exhortation to be used for the instruction of those seeking admission to the church. The
<u>Martyrdom of Perpetua</u>, however, is an exception to this rule
in that it is a first-hand account, the basic sections of
which are written by two of the martyrs, Perpetua and
Saturus, while a redactor supplies the introduction and
conclusion.[1]

We learn from the account that six friends were arrested in Carthage during the persecution by Septimius Severus
in 202-3. They were Vibia Perpetua, leader of the group and
daughter of a wealthy provincial; her slave, Felicitas, who
was eight months pregnant; Saturus, already a Christian and
the instructor of the others; Revocatus, Saturninus, and
Secundulus, three catechumens. The five recently instructed converts were baptized while under surveillance by the
authorities, and were jailed a few days later along with
their instructor.

While awaiting death, Perpetua was visited periodi-
cally by her pagan father and Christian relatives and
friends. All of them attempted without success to have her

recant for the sake of her aged father and young child whom she was still nursing. Convinced by her brother that she was in a position to ask God for a vision of her future, Perpetua did so and learned through four subsequent visions that: she was not to be freed, but was to prepare for martyrdom; her brother who had died some years previously was suffering and needed her help; her prayers and suffering released her brother from his affliction; and her victory as a martyr was assured.[2] The redactor's conclusion graphically portrays the actual events of the martyrs' deaths just as Perpetua had prophesied.

The account is of historical importance for a number of reasons. It is one of the earliest portrayals of Christian martyrdom as a powerful symbol of human liberation and self-fulfillment. As such it offers insights into the value system of an early Christian minority who through suffering and death gave witness to its ideal of truth. The account is punctuated with instances of the strong eschatological beliefs of this group. Herbert Musurillo concludes that the document's major import lies in the fact that it is both an account of the actual sufferings of the martyrs, and "an apocalypse in its own right".[3] The specific apocalyptic aspects are portrayed in the many visions the martyrs experienced before their death.[4]

As a portrayal of the vitality, zeal, and hopes of the early Christian community in North Africa, the account indicates principles which were to become a permanent part of the belief system of the African church. Because of its pervasive apocalyptic tenor and instances of belief in prophecy and direct divine inspiration, it reflects strong pro-Montanist tendencies. As such it suggests the reasons for Montanism's success in the West, and explains why "the hard, rigorist, martyr-inspired code which it represented should find a permanent place in the Christianity of North Africa and hence in the Western Church as a whole".[5] And since the martyrs were recent converts, the beliefs and aspirations reflected in their visions and behavior indicate current catechetical teaching, one of the more reliable indices of a group's basic tenets.[6]

The account helped establish the symbolism of Christian martyrdom for centuries to come, though it may itself have been influenced by earlier literature, particularly the

2

Shepherd of Hermas and the Apocalypse of Peter. Although
the Christian view of martyrdom was itself dependent to some
extent upon the views already held within the Jewish tradition, this in no way diminishes or denies the claim that many
later Christian martyr accounts were dependent either in content or form upon that of Perpetua.[7]

Another reason for the account's general historical
importance is its inclusion of two types of testimony. It
contains two first-person narrations of events as they
occurred or were predicted, and a redactor's third-person,
eye-witness claim of the veracity of those narrations. Such
verification by convergence of evidence rarely occurs within
one document.[8]

Equally rare is the fact that the central, most infor-
mative sections of the document are, in all probability,
written by a woman. This distinguishes it as the earliest
extant Christian literature written from a feminine viewpoint, a veritable rara avis among the male depictions of
women in past history. The account demonstrates the
emergence within the church of a prophetic movement in which
women assumed leadership roles indicative of a degree of
male/female equality unknown in later periods of Christian
history. It vividly portrays Perpetua's conscientious ob-
jections to certain restrictive elements within third-
century Carthaginian society, and symbolically suggests that
her liberation from these restrictions was accomplished
through a transcending of the expectations placed upon her
female sexuality. It is the two recurring themes, protest
and liberation, which explain the idealism prompting
Perpetua to make the choices she did, and which served as
inspiration and exhortation for future generations of
Christians. Furthermore, it is in the narration of Perpetua's forceful, but non-violent, series of protests that
one is able to discern the strong traits of her personality.

There is confirmation throughout the account that then,
as now, non-violent protest was generally considered a form
of disrespect for, and disobedience to, the norms of the
state, society, and family. For the Christian martyrs,
justification was derived from the theory that laws could
and ought to be defied for the sake of moral principles.
Final appeal was made to God as the highest authority.
Hence, protest was an integral part of the revolutionary

dynamic of martyrdom, especially when viewed in the light of
the apocalyptic and prophetic nature of the martyrs' faith.
Their faith accepted as certain the imminence of the end of
time. It filled its adherents with such courage, exaltation,
and anticipation of salvation that neither human punishment
nor earthly loyalty could destroy it. In such a context,
martyrdom served as the catalyst for the transformation of
an earthly, temporary life, to a heavenly, eternal one. For
the martyr, the rejection of earthly life was not so much a
looking forward to "a death which is the consummation of
vacuity, a final emptying of life into meaninglessness, but
towards a death which is the valid fulfillment of his existence".[9] It is this dual aspect of death which appears
within the Perpetua account; i.e., the finality of a less
acceptable form of life, and the beginning of a more glorious existence.

    Perpetua's protest took the form of a series of rejec-
tions made not for any lack of sensitivity or disregard for
the people involved, nor for any masochistic drive compelling
her to seek death. In fact, it is the record of her humane-
ness, her suffering because of anxiety and concern for others,
which makes the account such a compelling masterpiece. It is
apparent that her rejections were not so much negations of
contemporary reality, but affirmations and attestations of
her positive vision of a reality-to-be, the attainment of
which forced her to reject even those dearest to her. Her
rejections, nevertheless, were not without pain, particularly the rejection of her father and young child.[10]

    One of Perpetua's greatest sufferings while in prison,
is her inability to relieve the anxiety her father is
experiencing on her account. She states, "I was very upset
because of my father's condition. He was the only member
of my family who would find no reason for joy in my suffering".[11] She realizes that her father's motives in trying to
persuade her to recant were out of love for her, and she
responds with the repetitious, "I was sorry for my father's
sake.".[12] That the rejection of her father was painful, is
graphically portrayed in the confrontation with Hilarion,
the governor. When Perpetua appears before him and staunch-
ly refuses to pay homage to the gods of the state religion,
her father tries again to convince her of her folly. For
this interference the old man is thrown to the ground and
beaten with a rod, causing Perpetua such pain, "that I felt

as if I myself had been beaten. And I grieved because of
his pathetic old age."[13]   In their final meeting, her father,

> overwhelmed with grief, came again to
> see me. He began to pluck out his beard
> and throw it on the ground. Falling on his
> face before me, he cursed his old age, re-
> peating such things as would move all
> creation. And I grieved because of his
> unhappy old age.[14]

But in spite of her father's entreaties, Perpetua remains
firmly convinced that her rejections are justified and even
demanded by an appeal to a duty greater than that expected
of her as daughter. She reminds her father, "Whatever God
wants at this tribunal will happen, for remember that our
power comes not from ourselves but from God."[15]

The most compelling instances of her love and concern
for one whom she preferred but had to reject by precept, are
those dealing with the love for her child. After Perpetua
was imprisoned, she experienced great terror because of the
darkness, the heat, and the milling crowds. Her greatest
fear, however, was for the health and safety of her small
child.

> These were the trials I had to endure
> for many days. Then I was granted the
> privilege of having my son remain with
> me in prison. Being relieved of my
> anxiety and concern for the infant, I
> immediately regained my strength.
> Suddenly the prison became my palace,
> and I loved being there rather than any
> other place.[16]

But she ultimately had to reject her child who transformed
the prison existence for the short time that he was with
her. Several days before her martyrdom the infant was
given to her father who refused to return him to Perpetua.
She accepts this event as another of the many acts of the
providence of God, for "Then God saw to it that my child no
longer needed my nursing, nor were my breasts inflamed.
After that I was no longer tortured by anxiety about my
child".[17] The rejection effected a liberation towards a

5

higher goal, a liberation symbolized by the harmonious concurrence of Perpetua's peace of mind with health of body.

The authors of the text reject the generally held view of the prominent position accorded the Christian priesthood, particularly as it relates to the individual's pursuit of salvation. The individual's importance is derived from merit rather than position. In Saturus' vision, for example, Perpetua is invoked by a bishop and a priest to reconcile the differences between them. Although she acknowledges their superiority within the ecclesiastical hierarchy, she sees them standing outside the gates of heaven, clearly separated from the martyrs within. Their function is chiefly disciplinary since the bishop is chided by the angels to "Correct your people who flock to you as though returning from the games, fighting about the different teams."[18] Perpetua, as a martyr, is the sole instrument of her salvation, a belief symbolized in one of her visions by the ladder which was so narrow that "not more than one might ascend at a time."[19] She need not rely on a priest's mediation as she proceeds to reconcile herself with God and society: she can ask for visions on her own merit;[20] she has the necessary intercessory power to release her brother from his suffering;[21] as a lay-woman, she intercedes for a bishop and a priest;[22] and since the account intimates that martyrdom is a second baptism assuring salvation without priestly mediation, she can effect her salvation by direct combat with the powers of evil.[23]

So great was the martyr's power that one could converse directly with God, and be assured that the final death-agony could be endured because of Christ's presence within the martyr. This belief is poignantly expressed in the episode of Felicitas, the pregnant slave-girl. Since her pregnancy exempted her from martyrdom, she and the Christian prison community prayed that her baby be born prematurely. After concerted prayer, the labor pains began three days before the day of execution. As Felicitas groaned in childbirth, the jailer taunted her with, "If you're complaining now, what will you do when you'll be thrown to the wild beasts?" Felicitas replied, "Now it is I who suffer, but then another shall be in me to bear the pain for me, since I am now suffering for him."[24]

Perpetua rejected or ignored historical time. Her prophetic visions allowed her to concentrate on transcendence of time in a way that possibly only those liberated from the world and initiated into the mysteries of the Christ-model could experience. There was no longer for Perpetua the tension between time and the "substance of things hoped for," because she had already received that assurance in her vision. Her prophetic role presaged for herself and her friends in prison a new order arising from life bestowed at death. In her last recorded vision she indicates the strength of her desire to participate in the new order. While in combat with the devil disguised as an Egyptian, she felt herself being "lifted up into the air, and began to strike at him as one who was no longer earthbound."[25] And again, in Saturus' vision of the martyrs' arrival in heaven, Perpetua exclaims, "I thank God, for although I was happy on earth, I am much happier here right now."[26] It was this anticipation which allowed Perpetua to reject her family-community for the Christian prison-community who were united in the common hope of eternal life.

Perpetua rejected the demands of society by ultimately choosing death rather than the conventional form of loyalty to the Severan authorities. Her first priority was allegiance to Christ to whom she had made her commitment by becoming a Christian. She reminds her father that just as all things have their proper name according to their essence, "so I also cannot be called anything else than what I am, a Christian."[27] She publicly proclaims her Christian identity in the Forum before Hilarion the governor who condemns her to death for refusing to sacrifice to the gods of the state.[28]

One senses throughout the narrative the martyrs' attitude of definace and rebellion against authority. Apparently the powers of evil were personified in anyone attempting to dissuade the martyrs from loyalty to their faith. Perpetua in particular displays this attitude when, as leader of the group, she voices her protest against actions which she considered unjust or unduly repressive. Even her father whom she claimed to love dearly was severely judged because of his failure to understand her position. After one of many fierce disagreements with him, she informs us that "he left, overpowered by his diabolical arguments. For a few days my father stayed away. I thanked the Lord and felt relieved because of my father's absence."[29]

7

The powers of evil seemed particularly personified in the Roman rulers and officials, undoubtedly because then, as now, they epitomized the establishment. In fact, at times the change from the state religion to another was itself a protest against the established order. This defiance is exhibited by Perpetua as she protests the prisoners' mal-treatment by the jailers. She reminds a certain jailer that the prisoners deserve better food and quarters since anyone appearing publicly in the arena on the emperor's birthday (the day of their martydom), ought to be in good condition. The jailer, apparently unaccustomed to such boldness on the part of a woman, trembled, blushed, and gave orders that the prisoners be treated more humanely. He even allowed them to have visitors with whom they might dine.[30] On the day of martyrdom Perpetua was ordered to wear the women prisoners' customary dress of the priestess of Ceres. She argued effectively that if the prisoners were interested in con-forming to such regulations, they would undoubtedly not be in prison; and since they had devoted their lives to the cause of freedom they could not possibly acquiesce in such a re-quest during these last moments of life.[31]

The prisoners' view of martyrdom as ultimate victory allowed them to accept non-violence as a means of revenge against their persecutors. They need not take up arms against them since martyrdom itself was assurance of revenge hereafter when the positions of judge and judged would be reversed. On the evening before the martyrs' death a mob appeared at the prison to view the chief actors of the impending drama. The martyrs ridiculed their curiosity, and warned them of God's judgment. Saturus reprimanded them by asking, "Won't to-morrow's view be enough for you? Why are you so eager to see something you hate?...Take a good look so you'll recog-nize us on that day."[32] The following day as the prisoners marched past Hilarion, their motions and gestures indicated, "You condemn us; God condemns you," actions causing the mar-tyrs the added inconvenience of being publicly scourged. Un-daunted in their loyalty, "they rejoiced in that they had obtained yet another share in the Lord's suffering."[33]

In her last moments of life, Perpetua is given a final reminder of society's anti-feminine bias. The judge, con-sidered an instrument of the devil, "had readied a mad cow, an animal not usually used at these games, but selected so that the women's sex would be matched with that of the animal."[34] But Perpetua, in her final protest against the restrictive views of a male-dominated society, was not to be killed in such a manner. After she had been tossed by the mad cow,

> noticing that Felicitas was badly bruised, she went to her, reached out her hands and helped her to her feet...She (Perpetua) began to look around her, and to everyone's astonishment asked when they were going to be led out to the cow. She would not believe that it had already happened until she saw the various markings of the tossing on her body and clothing.[35]

Since the mad cow's attack did not kill her, she was to be executed in the usual manner, by the sword. Anticipating the beginning of the heavenly life which she had foreseen in her visions, Perpetua willingly participated in the completion of her martyrdom. When the novice swordsman was fumbling in the performance of his task, Perpetua "took his trembling hand and guided it to her throat."[36] The redactor adds the eulogistic note; "Perhaps it was that so great a woman, feared as she was by the unclean spirit, could not have been slain had she not herself willed it."[37]

Thus, the redactor completes the image of Perpetua, a woman whose self-liberation allowed her to transcend not only her expected role in society, but also the fear of death. Perpetua intimates in her actions and beliefs that for her, death was both the final liberation from the social injustices of her time, and the fulfillment of the promises of an eternal life of freedom. To some of Perpetua's contemporaries, her actions appeared as sheer madness; to others, like the redactor, they served as inspiration to join the martyrs in their protest.[38]

The point of view presented throughout the account is undoubtedly a woman's. There is repeated reference to childbearing, nursing, filial regard for father, maternal solicitude for son, concerns generally identified as female in nature. But to concentrate on these elements is to distort the image which Perpetua, Saturus, and the redactor present. The account is androgynous in that both feminine and masculine strands are evident, but they are so interwoven that

9

what emerges is a picture of humanity as a whole. The characters, both individually and collectively, stage their protest against those restrictions of state, society, and family which appear destructive of basic human freedom.

The martyr's conscious awareness of being first and foremost "Christian," and with God's help, "martyr," allowed little concern for traditional sex-role differentiation. Although Perpetua, for example, is the chief character in the events depicted, her actions are never detrimental to or pejorative of the male members of the group. The image which emerges of Perpetua, is that of the Christian female and male, the "every-person" of the early Christian Church in North Africa who aspired towards positive assurance of salvation. Therefore, Perpetua's solution for liberation from societal restrictions reflects a universal solution valid for men and women.

As symbol of the universal Christian, Perpetua's depiction in the role of both male and female intimates the early Christians' conviction that when the prophetic spirit breathes where it will there is no sexual preference. She is called bride, mother, sister, daughter, and lady; but also leader, warrior, victor, and fighter. She is at times gentle, womanly, kind, motherly, tender; at other times strong, fierce, daring, courageous. Perpetua is described in feminine terms as she walks from the prison to the arena on the day of martyrdom, "as a true spouse of Christ, the darling of God." But her countenance exhibits a masculine boldness and directness for "at her piercing glance all lowered their faces."[39] What is intimated here is best expressed by Perpetua herself as she recounts her last vision. She indicates that as she was about to battle with the Egyptian, "I was stripped of my clothing, and suddenly I was a man. My assistants began to rub me with oil as was the custom before a contest."[40] In keeping with the spirit of the narration it seems erroneous to interpret this as a belief in one's having to become a man in order to be saved. It is more consistent with the account to view it as symbolic of the necessity to prove oneself in battle before attaining the final prize. Since women were ordinarily not combatants in public games, both Perpetua's modesty and the metaphor's intent suffered less by Perpetua's male appearance. The trainer was apparently not deceived, for immediately after the battle he kissed her, and handed her the branch of victory saying, "Peace be with you, my daughter."[41] This section written by Perpetua is an appropriate climax to the androgynous account, in that Perpetua appears male in battle, female in victory. The female/male attributes are so intrinsic to her character that the sexual imagery can be interchanged without loss of essential significance.

Historical evidence indicates that the account's popularity spread rapidly throughout the church. Shortly after the original Latin version began its circulation, two other documents were produced from it; one in Greek, the other, a shorter Latin version which was generally used as part of the official church services. Archaeologists have proven that by the fourth century, if not before, a basilica at Carthage was dedicated to her memory, and the discovery of inscriptions indicate that she was well known at a fairly early date.[42] Augustine preached several sermons in her honor on March 7, the anniversary of her death, indicating his general knowledge of the account by quotes and paraphrases of the extant document.[43] Even two generations before Augustine, in the reign of Constantine, the anniversary of Perpetua's martyrdom appeared in the official calendar of the church at Rome.[44] Her name was subsequently inserted in the Canon of the Mass of the Latin Christian Church. Such a rapid development of the cult of Perpetua indicates her prominence among the early Christian martyr-saints. This then raises the question why this first-hand account, originally so well-known and widely used, was relatively unknown in later periods of Christian history.

Part of the answer may be that the earlier martyrs, who attained greater prominence, e.g., Ignatius of Antioch and Polycarp of Smyrna, were bishops. As such, they had greater influence in the churches, and were consequently better known. Ignatius wrote to the various churches and these letters were extensively circulated. Polycarp had the added distinction of being a disciple of St. John, whose place he assumed as head of the church at Smyrna. Also, if Tertullian was the redactor of Perpetua's account, his eventual rejection of and by the Christian Church at Rome because of his Montanist affiliation, may have cast doubt upon Perpetua's own loyalties to that church.[45]

The church's reversion to an essentially male hierarchical structure after the fourth or fifth century may partially explain the account's subsequent neglect. A document written by a woman may no longer have been considered proper or adequate for use in church services. The androgynous character of the account may have been overlooked when Perpetua's name was appended to it as the title. At any rate, the female strand was separated from the whole, and in a society which increasingly extolled the characteristics of maleness, the importance of an apparently female account was greatly diminished.

The significance of Perpetua's messages was similarly neglected in subsequent Christian history. The account represents a segment of early Christian society which allowed for equality in fact as well as in theory. As such, it stands in contradiction to the bulk of interpretative Christian literature, which views male dominance as an essential attribute of early Christian society. Perpetua's grasp of reality enabled her to view salvation as a release from the restrictive elements of an age, towards a life of irrevocable freedom. Without a doubt, the account allows the reader to conclude that when there is a question of essentials, (to change the words, but not the intent of Paul[46]) there are both male and female.

NOTES

1. The Latin original consists of twenty-one sections with four basic divisions:

   Sections 1- 2: Introduction by a redactor, possibly Tertullian

   Sections 3-10: Perpetua's prison diary; her personal account of the trials, experiences, visions in prison

   Sections 11-13: Saturus' description of his vision

   Sections 14-21: Redactor's conclusion; eye-witness narration of the actual martyrdom

   The majority of historians who have seriously studied the document, agree that Perpetua's and Saturus' accounts are authentic self-descriptions since they differ markedly from each other's and the redactor's style and use of language. For an analysis of the authorship of the various sections, cf. E.R. Dodds, Paganism and Christianity in an Age of Anxiety (Cambridge: University Press, 1965), pp. 49-52; E.C. Owen, Some Authentic Acts of the Early Martyrs (Oxford: Clarendon Press. 1927), pp. 74-77; J. Armitage Robinson, Texts and Studies I. No. 2 (Cambridge: University Press, 1891), pp. 43-58; W. H. Shewring, The Passion of Saints Perpetua and Felicity (London: Sheed and Ward, 1931), pp. xviii-xxiii. The most recent English translation is that of Herbert Musurillo, The Acts of the Christian Martyrs (Oxford: Clarendon Press, 1972), pp. 106-31.

2. Sections 4, 7, 8, 10.

3. Herbert Musurillo, Symbolism and the Christian Imagination (Baltimore: Helicon Press, 1962), p. 48.

4. For a Jungian analysis of Perpetua's visions, see Marie-Louise von Franz, "Die Passio Perpetua," in C.G. Jung, Aion (Zurich: Roscher, 1951), pp. 389-496. A recent interpretation of several of Perpetua's visions is contained in Mary R. Lefkowitz, "The Motivation for St.

Perpetua's Martyrdom," Journal of the American Academy of Religion, 44 (September, 1976), 417-21.

5. W.H.C. Frend, Martyrdom and Persecution in the Early Church: A Study of a Conflict from the Macabees to Donatus (Oxford: Basil Blackwell, 1965), p. 361. The Montanists followed the views of Montanus, a Phrygian enthusiast of the second century who claimed to have the Spirit dwelling within him. For further information about the sect, see Timothy David Barnes, Tertullian: A Historical and Literary Study (Oxford: Clarendon Press, 1971), pp. 131-142.

6. Some of the chief tenets of African Christianity evident in the account are (the numbers in parentheses indicating the specific sections of the text): individuals' direct access to gifts of prophecy and inspiration of the Spirit (1, 13); God's omniscience (5); the efficacy of prayers and sufferings of the living as atonement for the unrequited sins of the dead (7, 8); the devil as a powerful adversary (4); Christ's abiding presence within the martyr (15); martyrdom as a second baptism (18); the martyr as recipient of eternal reward, the martyr as recipient of eternal reward, the persecutor as recipient of eternal punishment (18); obedience to the will of God as man's first priority (3).

7. In a provocative study, Frend demonstrates how "the problem which the Christians posed to the Empire was fundamentally the same as that posed by Judaism, namely the reconciliation of the claims of a theocracy with those of a world empire." (op. cit., p. 22) Throughout his study he attempts to prove that the Christian view of martyrdom was in reality a prolongation, but also a superceding, of the views already held by Judaism. In regard to the later Christian accounts which relied upon that of the Perpetua, there are two especially, that of Marian and James, and Montanus and Lucius, which evidence intentional imitation. A comparative study of the accounts may be made from the following which contain all three accounts: Guiseppe Lazzati, Gli sviluppi della letteratura sui martiri nei primi quattro secoli (Torino: Societa Editrice Internazionale, 1956), pp. 177-213; Musurillo, Acts of the Christian Martyrs, pp. xxiii-xxxvii, and 194-239. Among the Perpetua

themes and symbols recurring most frequently in later accounts are: the ascent to heaven by means of a narrow ladder, the sides of which are affixed with sharp implements (4); the devil as adversary in the form of both men and beasts (4, 10, 20); the branch of victory (10); visions and dreams (4, 7, 8, 10, 11); angels as assistants to martyrs (11, 12); elders seated on a throne surrounded by angels (12); heaven as a garden (4, 11); celebration of the agape, love feast (17); martyrs' scorn of persecutors (15-18).

8. For further discussion of these two types of historical testimony and their importance in critical historical research, see William A. Clebsch, "History and Salvation: An Essay in Distinctions", The Study of Religion in Colleges and Universities, eds., Paul Ramsey and John F. Wilson (Princeton: University Press, 1960), pp. 56-7.

9. Karl Rahner, On the Theology of Death (New York: Herder and Herder, 1961), p. 87.

10. Neither Perpetua's nor Felicitas' husbands are mentioned in the account. Perpetua's anxiety for her father and son may stem from the fact that her father was non-Christian, and her son's chance of becoming a Christian was jeopardized by his being entrusted to her father. Consequently neither would be assured of salvation, and hence denied the eternal joys of heaven.

11. 5. The translation throughout is my own, derived from the Latin and Greek texts in Robinson, op. cit., pp. 60-95.

12. Idem. Cf. 3, 6, 9.

13. 6.

14. 9.

15. 5.

16. 3.

17. 6.

18. 13.

19. 4.

20. Idem.

21. 7, 8.

22. 13.

23. 18. Although Tertullian considered martyrdom a second baptism, it was probably not a general Christian belief till after the Decian persecution, around 250.

24. 15.

25. 10.

26. 12.

27. 3.

28. 6.

29. 3.

30. 16.

31. 18. Although there is no direct evidence of Perpetua's former participation in the cult of Ceres, we know that it was widespread throughout North Africa at this time. It is highly probable that certain distinctive features of the cult were incorporated into the martyrs' belief system; e.g., the belief in the individual's direct communication with divinity, the power of prophecy and woman's special role as prophetess, prayers for the dead, stress on the majestic aspects of divinity (those inculcating fear and dread), women's generally prominent position.

32. 17.

33. 18.

34. 20.

35. Idem.

36. 21.

37. Idem.

38. 16, 21.

39. 18.

40. 10.

41. Idem.

42. Ernest Diehl, Inscriptiones Latinae Christianae Veterae, I (Berlin: Weidmann, 1961), Nos. 2040a-41, p. 403. Cf. 1959a, 1962c, 3138 for slightly later inscriptions.

43. Sermons 280-2, appended to the translation of the Passio in Shewring, op. cit., pp. 45-59.

44. Perpetua's name appears in the Gelasian Sacramentary, ed., Henry Austin Wilson (Oxford: Clarendon Press, 1894), p. 168. The original sections of this book were probably compiled in the fifth century. It is highly probable that Perpetua's name already appeared at an earlier date in the Leonine Sacramentary, but since the first section (January-March) is not extant, no verification is possible. Ignatius of Antioch, a martyr who later became more prominent, was not mentioned in it either.

45. Although the account exhibits pro-Montanist tendencies there is no positive evidence of Perpetua's personal affiliation with the sect. Musurillo, op. cit., p. xxvi, concludes that "The phantasmagoric, and sometimes erotic, imagery, may well represent the kind of mediumistic phenomena current in the Montanist Church of Africa. However, the Montanist aspect of the work seems to have escaped the notice of Augustine and many of the early Fathers who admired its primitive charm and Christian fervour."

46. Gal. 3, 28; "there is neither male nor female".

17

THE MARTYRDOM OF PERPETUA

1. If instances of ancient faith which both testified to the grace of God and edified persons were written expressly for God's honor and humans' encouragement, why shouldn't recent events be similarly recorded for those same purposes? For these events will likewise become part of the past and vital to posterity, in spite of the fact that contemporary esteem for antiquity tends to minimize their value. And those who maintain that there is a single manifestation of the one Holy Spirit throughout the ages ought to consider that since a fullness of grace has been decreed for the last days of the world these recent events should be considered of greater value because of their proximity to those days. For "In the last days," says the Lord, "I shall diffuse my spirit over all humanity and their sons and daughters shall prophesy; the young shall see visions, and the old shall dream dreams."[1]

Just as we valued those prophecies so we acknowledge and reverence the new visions which were promised. And we consider the other powers of the Holy Spirit to be instruments of the Church to which that same Spirit was sent to administer all gifts to all people, just as the Lord allotted. For this reason we deem it necessary to disseminate the written accounts for the glory of God, lest anyone with a weak or despairing faith might think that supernatural grace prevailed solely among the ancients who were honored either by their experience of martyrdom or visions. For God always fulfills what he promises, either as proof to non-believers or as an added grace to believers.

And so, brothers and dear ones, we share with you those things which we have heard and touched with our hands,[2] so that those of you who were eye-witnesses of these deeds may be reminded of the glory of the Lord, and those of you now learning of it through this narration may associate yourselves with the holy martyrs and, through them, with the Lord Jesus Christ to whom there is glory and honor forever.[3] Amen.

2. Arrested were some young catechumens; Revocatus and Felicitas (both servants), Saturninus, Secundulus, and Vibia Perpetua, a young married woman about twenty years old, of

good family and upbringing.[4] She had a father, mother, two brothers (one was a catechumen like herself), and an infant son at the breast. The following account of her martyrdom is her own, a record in her own words of her perceptions of the event.

3.   While I was still with the police authorities (she said) my father out of love for me tried to dissuade me from my resolution. "Father," I said, "do you see here, for example, this vase, or pitcher, or whatever it is?" "I see it," he said. "Can it be named anything else than what it really is?", I asked, and he said, "No." "So I also cannot be called anything else than what I am, a Christian." Enraged by my words my father came at me as though to tear our my eyes. He only annoyed me, but he left, overpowered by his diabolical arguments.

For a few days my father stayed away. I thanked the Lord and felt relieved because of my father's absence. At this time we were baptized and the Spirit instructed me not to request anything from the baptismal waters except endurance of physical suffering.[5]

A few days later we were imprisoned. I was terrified because never before had I experienced such darkness. What a terrible day! Because of crowded conditions and rough treatment by the soldiers the heat was unbearable. My condition was aggravated by my anxiety for my baby. Then Tertius and Pomponius, those kind deacons who were taking care of our needs, paid for us to be moved for a few hours to a better part of the prison where we might refresh ourselves. Leaving the dungeon we all went about our own business. I nursed my child, who was already weak from hunger. In my anxiety for the infant I spoke to my mother about him, tried to console my brother, and asked that they care for my son.[6] I suffered intensely because I sensed their agony on my account. These were the trials I had to endure for many days. Then I was granted the privilege of having my son remain with me in prison. Being relieved of my anxiety and concern for the infant, I immediately regained my strength. Suddenly the prison became my palace, and I loved being there rather than any other place.

4.   Then my brother said to me, "Dear sister, you already have such a great reputation that you could ask for

a vision indicating whether you will be condemned or freed." Since I knew that I could speak with the Lord, whose great favors I had already experienced, I confidently promised to do so. I said I would tell my brother about it the next day. Then I made my request and this is what I saw.

There was a bronze ladder of extraordinary height reaching up to heaven, but it was so narrow that only one person could ascend at a time.[7] Every conceivable kind of iron weapon was attached to the sides of the ladder: swords, lances, hooks, and daggers. If anyone climbed up carelessly or without looking upwards, he/she would be mangled as the flesh adhered to the weapons. Crouching directly beneath the ladder was a monstrous dragon who threatened those climbing up and tried to frighten them from ascent.

Saturus went up first. Because of his concern for us he had given himself up voluntarily after we had been arrested. He had been our source of strength but was not with us at the time of the arrest).[8] When he reached the top of the ladder he turned to me and said, "Perpetua, I'm waiting for you, but be careful not to be bitten by the dragon." I told him that in the name of Jesus Christ the dragon could not harm me. At this the dragon slowly lowered its head as though afraid of me. Using its head as the first step, I began my ascent."

At the summit I saw an immense garden, in the center of which sat a tall, grey-haired man dressed like a shepherd, milking sheep. Standing around him were several thousand white-robed people. As he raised his head he noticed me and said, "Welcome, my child." Then he beckoned me to approach and gave me a small morsel of the cheese he was making. I accepted it with cupped hands and ate it. When all those surrounding us said "Amen," I awoke, still tasting the sweet cheese. I immediately told my brother about the vision, and we both realized that we were to experience the sufferings of martyrdom. From then on we gave up having any hope in this world.

5. A few days later there was a rumor that our case was to be heard. My father, completely exhausted from his anxiety, came from the city to see me, with the intention of weakening my faith. "Daughter", he said, "have pity on my grey head. Have pity on your father if I have the honor to

be called father by you, if with these hands I have brought
you to the prime of your life, and if I have always favored
you above your brothers, do not abandon me to the reproach
of men. Consider your brothers; consider your mother and
your aunt; consider your son who cannot live without you.
Give up your stubbornness before you destroy all of us.
None of us will be able to speak freely if anything happens
to you."

These were the things my father said out of love, kissing
my hands and throwing himself at my feet. With tears he called
me not daughter, but woman. I was very upset because of my
father's condition. He was the only member of my family who
would find no reason for joy in my suffering. I tried to
comfort him saying, "Whatever God wants at this tribunal will
happen, for remember that our power comes not from ourselves
but from God." But utterly dejected, my father left me.

6. One day as we were eating we were suddenly rushed
off for a hearing. We arrived at the forum and the news
spread quickly throughout the area near the forum, and a
huge crowd gathered. We went up to the prisoners' platform.
All the others confessed when they were questioned. When
my turn came my father appeared with my son. Dragging me
from the step, he begged: "Have pity on your son!"

Hilarion, the governor, who assumed power after the
death of the proconsul Minucius Timinianus,[9] said, "Have pity
on your father's grey head; have pity on your infant son;
offer sacrifice for the emperors' welfare". But I answered,
"I will not." Hilarion asked, "Are you a Christian?" And
I answered, "I am a Christian." And when my father persisted
in his attempts to dissuade me, Hilarion ordered him thrown
out, and he was beaten with a rod. My father's injury hurt
me as much as if I myself had been beaten, and I grieved because of his pathetic old age. Then the sentence was passed;
all of us were condemned to the beasts. We were overjoyed
as we went back to the prison cell. Since I was still nursing my child who was ordinarily in the cell with me, I
quickly sent the deacon Pomponius to my father's house to ask
for the baby, but my father refused to give him up. Then
God saw to it that my child no longer needed my nursing, nor
were my breasts inflamed. After that I was no longer tortured by anxiety about my child or by pain in my breasts.

22

7. A few days later while all of us were praying, in the middle of a prayer I suddenly called out the name "Dinocrates." I was astonished since I hadn't thought about him till then. When I recalled what had happened to him I was very disturbed and decided right then that I had not only the right, but the obligation, to pray for him. So I began to pray repeatedly and to make moaning sounds to the Lord in his behalf. During that same night I had this vision: I saw Dinocrates walking away from one of many very dark places. He seemed very hot and thirsty, his face grimy and colorless. The wound on his face was just as it had been when he died. This Dinocrates was my blood-brother who at the age of seven died very tragically from a cancerous disease which so disfigured his face that his death was repulsive to everyone. It was for him that I now prayed. But neither of us could reach the other because of the great distance between. In the place where Dinocrates stood was a pool filled with water, and the rim of the pool was so high that it extended far above the boy's height. Dinocrates stood on his toes as if to drink the water but in spite of the fact that the pool was full, he could not drink because the rim was so high!

I realized that my brother was in trouble, but I was confident that I could help him with his problem. I prayed for him every day until we were transferred to the arena prison where we were to fight wild animals on the birthday of Geta Caesar.[11] And I prayed day and night for him, moaning and weeping so that my petition would be granted.

8. On the day that we were kept in chains, I had the following vision: I saw the same place as before, but Dinocrates was clean, well-dressed, looking refreshed. In place of the wound there was a scar, and the fountain which I had seen previously now had its rim lowered to the boy's waist. On the rim, over which water was flowing constantly, there was a golden bowl filled with water. Dinocrates walked up to it and began to drink; the bowl never emptied. And when he was no longer thirsty, he gladly went to play as children do. Then I awoke, knowing that he had been relieved of his suffering.

9. A few days passed. Pudens, the official in charge of the prison (the official who had gradually come to admire us for our persistence), admitted many prisoners to our cell so that we might mutually encourage each other. As the day

of the games drew near, my father, overwhelmed with grief,
came again to see me. He began to pluck out his beard and
throw it on the ground. Falling on his face before me, he
cursed his old age, repeating such things as would move all
creation. And I grieved because of his old age.

10.   The day before the battle in the arena, in a vision
I saw Pomponius the deacon coming to the prison door and
knocking very loudly. I went to open the gate for him. He
was dressed in a loosely fitting white robe, wearing richly
decorated sandals. He said to me, "Perpetua, come. We're
waiting for you!" He took my hand and we began to walk over
extremely rocky and winding paths. When we finally arrived
short of breath, at the arena, he led me to the center saying,
"Don't be frightened! I'll be here to help you." He left
me and I stared out over a huge crown which watched me with
apprehension. Because I knew that I had to fight with the
beasts, I wondered why they hadn't yet been turned loose in
the arena. Coming towards me was some type of Egyptian,
horrible to look at, accompanied by fighters who were to
help defeat me. Some handsome young men came forward to
help and encourage me. I was stripped of my clothing, and
suddenly I was a man. My assistants began to rub me with
oil as was the custom before a contest, while the Egyptian
was on the opposite side rolling in the sand. Then a
certain man appeared, so tall that he towered above the
amphitheatre. He wore a loose purple robe with two parallel
stripes across the chest; his sandals were richly decorated
with gold and silver. He carried a rod like that of an
athletic trainer, and a green branch on which were golden
apples. He motioned for silence and said, "If this Egyptian
wins, he will kill her with the sword; but if she wins, she
will receive this branch." Then he withdrew.

We both stepped forward and began to fight with our
fists. My opponent kept trying to grab my feet but I repeatedly kicked his face with my heels. I felt myself being
lifted up into the air and began to strike at him as one who
was no longer earth-bound. But when I saw that we were
wasting time, I put my two hands together, linked my fingers,
and put his head between them. As he fell on his face I
stepped on his head. Then the people began to shout and my
assistants started singing victory songs. I walked up to the
trainer and accepted the branch.[12] He kissed me and said,
"Peace be with you, my daughter." And I triumphantly headed

24

towards the Sanavivarian Gate.[13] Then I woke up realizing
that I would be contending not with wild animals but with
the devil himself. I knew, however, that I would win. I
have recorded the events which occurred up to the day before
the final contest. Let anyone who wishes to record the
events of the contest itself, do so."

11. The saintly Saturus also related a vision which he
had and it is recorded here in his own hand. Our suffering
had ended (he said), and we were being carried towards the
east by four angels whose hands never touched us. And we
floated upward, not in a supine position, but as though we
were climbing a gentle slope. As we left the earth's
atmosphere we saw a brilliant light, and I said to Perpetua
who was at my side, "This is what the Lord promised us. We
have received his promise."

And while we were being carried along by those four
angels we saw a large open space like a splendid garden
landscaped with rose trees and every variety of flower.
The trees were as tall as cypresses whose leaves rustled
gently and incessantly. And there in that garden-sanctuary
were four other angels, more dazzling than the rest. And
when they saw us they showed us honor, saying to the other
angels in admiration, "Here they are! They have arrived."

And those four angels who were carrying us began trembling
in awe and set us down. And we walked through a violet-
strewn field where we met Jocundus, Saturninus, and Artaxius
who were burned alive in that same persecution, and Quintus,
also a martyr, who had died in prison. We were asking them
where they had been, when the other angels said to us,
"First, come this way. Go in and greet the Lord."

12. We went up to a place where the walls seemed constructed of light. At the entrance of the place stood four
angels who put white robes on those who entered. We went in
and heard a unified voice chanting endlessly, "Holy, holy,
holy." We saw a white haired man sitting there who, in
spite of his snowy white hair, had the features of a young
man. His feet were not visible. On his right and left were
four elderly gentlemen and behind them stood many more. As
we entered we stood in amazement before the throne. Four
angels supported us as we went up to kiss the aged man, and
he gently stroked our faces with his hands. The other
elderly men said to us, "Stand up." We rose and gave the

25

kiss of peace. Then they told us to enjoy ourselves. I
said to Perpetua, "You have your wish." She answered, "I
thank God, for although I was happy on earth, I am much
happier here right now."

13. Then we went out, and before the gates we saw
Optatus the bishop on the right and Aspasius the priest and
teacher on the left, both looking sad as they stood there
separated from each other. They knelt before us saying,
"Make peace between us, for you've gone away and left us
this way." But we said to them "Aren't you our spiritual
father, and our teacher? Why are you kneeling before us?"
We were deeply touched and we embraced them. And Perpetua
began to speak to them in Greek and we invited them into the
garden beneath a rose tree. While we were talking with them,
the angels said to them, "Let them refresh themselves, and
if you have any dissensions among you, forgive one another."
This disturbed both of them and the angels said to Optatus,
"Correct your people who flock to you as though returning
from the games, fighting about the different teams." It
seemed to us that they wanted to close the gates, and there
we began to recognize many of our friends, among whom were
martyrs. We were all sustained by an indescribable fragrance
which completely satisfied us. Then in my joy, I awoke.

14. The remarkable visions narrated above were those
of the blessed martyrs Saturus and Perpetua, just as they
put them in writing. As for Secundulus, while he was still
in prison God gave him the grace of an earlier exit from
this world, so that he could escape combat with the wild
beasts. But his body, though not his soul, certainly felt
the sword.

15. As for Felicitas, she too was touched by God's
grace in the following manner. She was pregnant when
arrested, and was now in her eighth month. As the day of
the contest approached she became very distressed that her
martyrdom might be delayed, since the law forbade the execution of a pregnant woman. Then she would later have to shed
her holy and innocent blood among common criminals. Her
friends in martyrdom were equally sad at the thought of
abandoning such a good friend to travel alone on the same
road to hope.

And so, two days before the contest, united in grief

they prayed to the Lord. Immediately after the prayers her labor pains began. Because of the additional pain natural for an eighth-month delivery, she suffered greatly during the birth, and one of the prison guards taunted her; "If you're complaining now, what will you do when you'll be thrown to the wild beasts? You didn't think of them when you refused to sacrifice." She answered, "Now it is I who suffer, but then another shall be in me to bear the pain for me, since I am now suffering for him." And she gave birth to a girl whom one of her sisters reared as her own daughter.

16. Since the Holy Spirit has permitted, and by permitting has willed, that the events of the contest be recorded, we have no choice but to carry out the injunction (rather, the sacred trust) of Perpetua, in spite of the fact that it will be an inferior addition to the magnificent events already described. We are adding an instance of Perpetua's perseverance and lively spirit. At one time the prisoners were being treated with unusual severity by the commanding officer because certain deceitful men had intimated to him that the prisoners might escape by some magic spells. Perpetua openly challenged him; "Why don't you at least allow us to freshen up, the most noble of the condemned, since we belong to Caesar and are about to fight on his birthday? Or isn't it to your credit that we should appear in good condition on that day?" The officer grimaced and blushed, then ordered that they be treated more humanely and that her brothers and others be allowed to visit and dine with them. By this time the prison warden was himself a believer.

17. On the day before the public games, as they were eating the last meal commonly called the free meal, they tried as much as possible to make it instead an agape.[14] In the same spirit they were exhorting the people, warning them to remember the judgment of God, asking them to be witnesses to the prisoners' joy in suffering, and ridiculing the curiosity of the crowd. Saturus told them, "Won't tomorrow's view be enough for you? Why are you so eager to see something you hate? Friends today, enemies tomorrow! Take a good look so you'll recognize us on that day." Then they all left the prison amazed, and many of them began to believe.

27

18. The day of their victory dawned, and with joyful
countenances they marched from the prison to the arena as
though on their way to heaven. If there was any trembling
it was from joy, not fear. Perpetua followed with quick
step as a true spouse of Christ, the darling of God, her
brightly flashing eyes quelling the gaze of the crowd.
Felicitas too, joyful because she had safely survived child-
birth and was now able to participate in the contest with
the wild animals, passed from one shedding of blood to
another; from midwife to gladiator, about to be purified
after child-birth by a second baptism. As they were led
through the gate they were ordered to put on different
clothes; the men, those priests of Saturn, the women, those
of the priestesses of Ceres. But that noble woman stubborn-
ly resisted even to the end. She said, "We've come this
far voluntarily in order to protect our rights, and we've
pledged our lives not to recapitulate on any such matter as
this. We made this agreement with you." Injustice bowed
to justice and the guard conceded that they could enter the
arena in their ordinary dress. Perpetua was singing victory
psalms as if already crushing the head of the Egyptian.
Revocatus, Saturninus and Saturus were warning the specta-
tors, and as they came within sight of Hilarion they informed him by nods and gestures: "You condemn us; God condemns
you." This so infuriated the crowds that they demanded the
scourging of these men in front of the line of gladiators.
But the ones so punished rejoiced in that they had obtained
yet another share in the Lord's suffering.

19. Whoever said, "Ask and you shall receive,"
granted to these petitioners the particular death that each
one chose. For whenever the martyrs were discussing among
themselves their choice of death, Saturus used to say that
he wished to be thrown in with all the animals so that he
might wear a more glorious crown. Accordingly, at the out-
set of the show he was matched against a leopard but then
called back; then he was mauled by a bear on the exhibition
platform. Now Saturus detested nothing as much as a bear
and he had already decided to die by one bite from the
leopard. Consequently, when he was tied to a wild boar the
professional gladiator who had tied the two together was
pierced instead and died shortly after the games ended,
while Saturus was merely dragged about. And when he was
tied up on the bridge in front of the bear, the bear refused to come out of his den; and so a second time Saturus

28

was called back unharmed.

20. For the young women the devil had readied a mad cow, an animal not usually used at these games, but selected so that the women's sex would be matched with that of the animal. After being stripped and enmeshed in nets, the women were led into the arena. How horrified the people were as they saw that one was a young girl and the other, her breasts dripping with milk, had just recently given birth to a child. Consequently both were recalled and dressed in loosely fitting gowns.

Perpetua was tossed first and fell on her back. She sat up, and being more concerned with her sense of modesty than with her pain, covered her thighs with her gown which had been torn down one side. Then finding her hair-clip which had fallen out, she pinned back her loose hair thinking it not proper for a martyr to suffer with dishevelled hair; it might seem that she was mourning in her hour of triumph. Then she stood up. Noticing that Felicitas was badly bruised, she went to her, reached out her hands and helped her to her feet. As they stood there the cruelty of the crowds seemed to be appeased and they were sent to the Sanavivarian Gate. There Perpetua was taken care of by a certain catechumen, Rusticus, who stayed near her. She seemed to be waking from a deep sleep (so completely had she been entranced and imbued with the Spirit). She began to look around her and to everyone's astonishment asked, "When are we going to be led out to that cow, or whatever it is." She would not believe that it had already happened until she saw the various markings of the tossing on her body and clothing. Then calling for her brother she said to him and to the catechumen, "Remain strong in your faith and love one another. Do not let our excruciating sufferings become a stumbling block for you."

21. Meanwhile, at another gate Saturus was similarly encouraging the soldier, Pudens. "Up to the present," he said, "I've not been harmed by any of the animals, just as I've foretold and predicted. So that you will now believe completely, watch as I go back to die from a single leopard bite." And so at the end of that contest, Saturus was bitten once by the leopard that had been set loose, and bled so profusely from that one wound that as he was coming back the crowd shouted in witness to his second baptism: "Sal-

vation by being cleansed; Salvation by being cleansed;"[15]
And that man was truly saved who was cleansed in this way.

Then Saturus said to Pudens the soldier, "Goodbye, and
remember my faith. Let these happenings be a source of
strength for you, rather than a cause for anxiety." Then
asking Pudens for a ring from his finger, he dipped it into
the wound and returned it to Pudens as a legacy, a pledge
and remembrance of his death. And as he collapsed he was
thrown with the rest to that place reserved for the usual
throat-slitting. And when the crowd demanded that the
prisoners be brought out into the open so that they might
feast their eyes on death by the sword, they voluntarily
arose and moved where the crowd wanted them. Before doing
so they kissed each other so that their martyrdom would be
completely perfected by the rite of the kiss of peace.

The others, without making any movement or sound, were
killed by the sword. Saturus in particular, since he had
been the first to climb the ladder and was to be Perpetua's
encouragement, was the first to die. But Perpetua, in order
to feel some of the pain, groaning as she was struck between
the ribs, took the gladiator's trembling hand guided it to
her throat. Perhaps it was that so great a woman, feared
as she was by the unclean spirit, could not have been slain
had she not herself willed it.

O brave and fortunate martyrs, truly called and chosen
to give honor to our Lord Jesus Christ! And anyone who is
elaborating upon, or who reverences or worships that honor,
should read these more recent examples, along with the
ancient, as sources of encouragement for the Christian community. In this way, there will be new examples of courage
witnessing to the fact that even in our day the same Holy
Spirit is still efficaciously present, along with the all
powerful God the Father and Jesus Christ our Lord, to whom
there will always be glory and endless power. Amen.

NOTES

1. Acts 2:17-18. Cf. Joel 2:28.

2. I John 1:3. Cf. 1 Cor. 7:17; Rom. 12:3.

3. I John 1:3.

4. A catechumen was one receiving instruction in the basic beliefs and teachings of the Christian faith prior to baptism.

5. Apparently after baptism the newly baptized could pray for a special grace or gift. Cf. Tertullian, De Bapt. 20.

6. From the rest of the account it appears that Perpetua's mother was bringing the child to and from prison.

7. Cf. Jacob's ladder in Gen. 28:12.

8. Since Saturus was not listed as a catechumen he was probably the instructor of the others prior to their arrest.

9. There is no real information about Minucius Timianus, but Hilarion is mentioned as an African proconsul by Tertullian, Ad Scapulam 3.1. Hilarion was evidently temporarily serving as governor until a new one would be appointed.

10. The reason Dinocrates was unable to drink the water may have been due to his dying before being baptized. Augustine (De Anima 1.12) maintained that the boy had committed sins after baptism and had not been cleansed of those sins prior to death.

11. This incidental reference to the celebration of games on Geta's birthday helps establish the date of the martrydom somewhere between 200-205.

12. The branch was the reward presented to the victor in any kind of official combat or contest.

13. The Porta Sanavivaria (Gate of Life) was the gate by
    which the victors would exit. Those who were defeated
    were carried out through the Porta Libitinensis.

14. The agape or "love feast" was the common meal shared by
    the early Christian communities. It was the visible
    expression of the love Christians felt for each other
    as co-sharers of the love of Christ.

15. One of the customary greetings of good omen before and
    after the public baths was "Salvum lotum," here used
    ironically by the crowd in the amphitheater.

PROBA CENTO

Life

Line twelve of the cento identifies the author as one
"Proba." Who was Proba? What was her station in life and
her relation to the faith?

The oldest monastic codices all list the author of the
cento as simply "Proba." Later ones list her as Faltonia
Proba; others as Falconia Proba. All the records we possess
of her life testify that she was a Roman matron whose family,
the Anicii, was distinguised in several generations by members who held consultates and praefectures which, in the Late
Empire, admitted one to the clarissimate, the senatorial
class, and to the first order of precedence within that class.
Proba's character was respectable and dignified, and, some
sources specify, generous. She may have been a convert to
Christianity in midlife. There is no evidence to support
that she was other than a lay woman who did not choose the
ascetic life for which a small number of aristocratic women
had a vocation. Proba as a matron of the gens Anicii lived
the life common to a woman of the Roman privileged class,
great leisure; one she used for what was considered by her
class to be both a duty and a pleasure, a close and careful
study of the classical writers, especially Vergil.

There is a century old debate among scholars and critics
concerning which one of the several women named "Proba"
within the Anicii family tree is the one referred to by the
foregoing character sketch.

In 1870 Joseph Aschbach after extensive work on the
stemma of the Anicii, and after reconsideration of the references to Proba in Isidore of Seville, maintained that Isidore's
identification of Proba as the wife of Proconsul Adelphius was
in error. Aschbach asserted that Isidore, known to be a less
than a factually oriented historian, incorrectly interpolated
the identity of the creator of the cento from a distance of
three centuries by using corrupted inscriptions.

There was, Aschbach maintained, a Falconia Proba who was
the wife of the proconsul Adelphius, a man who had previously
been the city prefect of Horta, 50 miles N.W. of Rome (near

Viterbo). But this Falconia Proba was not the author of the Cento, but the mother of Olybrius Adelphius Probus, proconsul of Africa, who was the father of Faltonia Proba. It was this younger Proba, granddaughter of Falconia Proba who was the author of our Cento Vergilianus.[1]

Carol Schenkl in 1880 in his standard annotated, critical edition of the Cento argued that Isidore had been correct all along: Proba, the author of the work, was the wife of proconsul Clodius Celsinus Adelphius, prefect in 351 AD for one half year. Her grandfather, Probus, was consul in 310 AD as was her father Petronius Probianus in 322 AD (and perhaps her brother in 341). Her son, Olybrius, was consul in 379 and prefect in 391. Her nephew, Petronius Probus, prefect of Illyricum, Italy, and Africa in the 380's was one of the richest men in the Empire and is remembered for his ruthless fiscal exploitation through taxation, seizure, and extortion of the members of his own class. He married Proba's granddaughter Faltonia whom Schaff and Kelly identify as the "Lady Proba" to whom Augustine wrote letters.

Schenkl supported his argument with a tenth century Benedictine manuscript which refers to "Proba, wife of Adelphius, mother of Olybrius and Aliepius, who wrote this cento while Constantius fought against Magnetius." He further pointed up what he considered to be errors in Aschbach's supporting documents, citing misspellings which led to mix-ups in the names of fathers and sons.[2]

Unfortunately neither argument is fully grounded in well-attested manuscripts, and none of the documents is readily available. Some in fact, were destroyed in the 1700's, and even Schenkl and Aschbach were working from secondary sources and notes. Consequently the dating of the cento is uncertain. Schenkl, on the authority of the Benedictine manuscript mentioned above dated the cento around 351 AD. Aschbach dated it around 379 to correspond to the reign of the Emperors referred to in his documentary sources. Labriolle skirts the issue in his survey by designating the date of composition "second half of the fourth century".[3] My own preference is to follow Schenkl for in her prologue Proba refers to a civil war in which "fair shields", i.e., family standards, were "stained with parent's blood." This description would better fit the situation of the state in the year 351 at the culmination of

the series of conflicts for the succession begun by
Constantine rather than the events in 379. The document which
Schenkl cited mentions the war between Constantius and
Magnetius, but that may be the result of an incorrect 10th
century speculation as to the antecedent Proba is referring
to with her own phrase "civil wars." Aschbach argued that
the war was that between Constantine and Maxentius.

The date of 351 AD (361 at the latest), seems the most
likely one for this work of Proba. It may be that she began
writing it at the earlier time in response to the conflict
between the old and new religion within her own class, an
aristocracy which welcomed Julian the Apostate to imperial
office; she may have finished it only after Julian's edict
barring Christians from teaching rhetoric which thus made
her cento a necessity. Indeed, if she did not begin it
until then, the reference to the civil wars as having taken
place in "times long past" might be explained.

The act of Proba in writing her cento had a radical
character during this period. Although the legal and social
status of aristocratic women had been steadily improving
throughout Graceo-Roman antiquity to the extent that a
woman "entered her husband's home of her own free will and
lived in it as his equal",4 matters in the church were
different. As a tool for fulfilling what Jerome subsequently
called one of the ideals of marriage, the education of the
new generation; her cento contributed in a small part to the
greater social revolution occurring in her time. In the act
of authorship Proba claimed a self-assertive identity in a
Christian community which was guided by the church fathers'
interpretations of Paul which forbade women from doing
theology.

> Against the widespread theological apologetics
> which argues that the church could not liberate
> women because of the culturally inferior position
> of women in antiquity, it has to be pointed out
> that the cultural and societal emancipation of
> women had gained considerable ground in the Graeco-
> Roman world. Paul, the post-Paul tradition, and
> the Church fathers, therefore, not only attempted
> to limit or eliminate the consequences of the actions
> of Jesus and of the Spirit. . .but also reversed the
> repression and elimination of the emancipatory

processes of their society. . .hand in hand with
the repression and elimination of the emancipatory
elements within the Church went a theological
justification for such oppression of women.[5]

Whether her cento was one of the many that were produced by
women her equal or one unique creative outburst of a devoted
individual woman, the cento is the memorial of the "no"
that some women of the early years of the church said to the
church's attempt to obliterate and subliminate their dignity
as persons who are, with their fellows, one in the body of
Christ.

Work

The cento as Proba employed it grew out of a veneration
for a particular poet, Vergil, (but sometimes Ovid) in the
West, and Homer in the East. Comparetti identifies two
reasons for the rise of the cento. First, there was great
familiarity with Vergil's writings in the West, even if
they had been only mechanically learned; and second, there
was a "poverty of ideas" in secular literary circles which
led would-be authors to emulate the great master.[6]

The form itself is one wherein the author-redactor
creates a new work by piecing together complete lines and
half-lines of another poet to form a mosaic. To us today
this may seem like a tedious and foolish effort at plagiar-
ism, but in the centuries of the Empire, such use of another's
work was seen, according to Comparetti, as the highest mode
of praise for that author. "Pseudographia" and unattributed
quotations abound in Christian and secular literature of the
time.

Ordinarily a vergilian cento uses lines from the Eclogues,
Georgics, and the Aeneid although lines might be taken from
only one or two works. These lines were "twisted more or
less skillfully into meanings quite unforeseen by the bard
of Mantua."[7]

Cento poetry was widely fashionable in the fourth century. It was, however, in existence before the time of
Tertullian (200 AD) when he wrote:

We see today issuing from Vergil some entirely
different fable in which the subject is adapted
to verse and the verse to the subject. Hosidius
Geta "pumped up" his entire _Medea_ from Vergil!8

Proba, according to Isidaore of Seville seventh century bishop
and encyclopedist, was the initiator of the Christian cento
tradition.

Within a short time after her writing of the _Cento_, it
was held in high repute. Caesar Arcadius requested a copy,
and the dedicatory poem (lines 1-23) commonly prefixed to
the _Cento_ was written at that time by a hand other than
Proba's.

Two subsequent Christian works show traces of her influence. Pomponius' _Dialogue of Tityrus and Meliboeus_ is
quite obviously fashioned after the _Eclogues_, and its content is a basic course in the Christian mythos. It includes
a discussion of the nature and power of God, the immortality
of the soul, and a condensed biblical narrative. It is in
those sections covering the Creation, Fall, and Salvation in
Christ that one finds the same Vergilian lines and combina-
tions that Proba used in describing those identical events.
A late poetic work (526 AD) by Avitus, _De mosaicae historiae
gestis libri quinque_, is not a cento but may also have been
influenced by Proba. The Old Testament salvation history
set forth by Avitus is similar in order, content, and treatment to Proba's accounts of the Creation, Fall, Expulsion
from the Garden, Deluge, and Crossing of the Red Sea.9

Despite harsh comments by Jerome (Ep. 130) and a decree
by Gelasius, Bishop of Rome, in 496 AD which relegated the
Cento of Proba to the "apocryphal" writings (which were to
be used only for private reading), the _Cento_ remained a
popular work as a school text well into the Middle Ages. Its
presence is attested to in the catalogues of many monastic
libraries through the 12th century, often being bound with
Aldhelm's _Symposia_ and _Enigmas_, poems of Cyprian, Gregory,
and Forunatus, or with works of Adelard and Seneca: all of
which were used in the instruction of boys.

The _Probae Cento_ proper opens with an exploration of
why the poem is being written. Once, while still a pagan,
Proba had written of civil war (1.24 f.), but since her

conversion to Chrsit she wishes to sing the "gentle gifts of Christ." After line 38 she implies that she will write a story Christ to show that the Old Testament is fulfilled in the Incarnation.

The first section of the poem ends at line 333. It is an epitome of the Old Testament: Creation, Fall including effects in nature, Death of Abel, and the Deluge. An abbreviated version of the Exodus and the giving of the laws end this part.

The creation of the earth and the creatures is a section of sheer delight for Proba appropriately uses vibrant images from the Georgics, a work which extolls the variety and beauty of nature. She follows the events of Genesis 1.

At line 333 Proba breaks off the narrative and explains that she is going to skip the rest of the Old Testament because we all know it anyhow and she wishes to move onto the more important stories of the faith (1. 333-345). One gets the sense that she suddenly feels that she has bitten off more than she wants to chew and that she is frustrated by the paucity of lines and half-lines in which there are images transferable from Vergil. This sense is reinforced by the spotty quality of the stories which follow. A rough harmony of Matthew and Mark with Lucan insertions includes a reference to the prophecies, Jesus' birth (1. 346 f.), the arrival of the kings and the slaughter of the innocents (1. 352 f.), the flight into Egypt (1.370 f.), the baptism and teachings (1. 400 f.), the young rich ruler (1. 505 f.), the storm on the lake (1. 513 f.), the procession into Jerusalem and the cleansing of the Temple (1. 571 f.), the Last Supper (1. 599 f.), the Passion (1. 600 f.), and the Ascension.

Her skill in adapting Vergil to the evangelical stories is evident in the tale of the slaughter of the innocents, one of the clearer New Testament passages in the last half of the cento which flows smoothly and concisely with touches of naturalistic deatil. Although the Scriptures do not say in what manner the children were slain, Proba attributes their destruction to fire (1. 36). This is an appropriate use of a Greek image, however, for fire was often the symbol of irrational passion. It was such passion in Herod that killed the children.

After this chilling scene and a mention of the flight to Egypt, Proba follows with an idyllic humn to the infant Jesus safely in Egypt (1. 377-379), his cradle filled with blossoms and surrounded by the holy and aromatic trees of the land. The slaughter, as a metaphor for the human condition with its proclivity towards evil, is, in a sense, followed by metaphors of salvation, peace, and joy; all of which surround the Christ and those who have fled to a new land with him.

In other parts of the cento Proba is not so successful. Like the Flight, the Last Supper (1. 599) is grammatically and symbolically awkward. In her retelling of the life of Jesus, she omits large portions of his ministry and abbreviates the stories that she does use drastically. This severe editing of the Gospel stories, plus the fact that one often must juxtapose the Scriptures to the text in order to follow her train of thought would seem to render the Cento clear only to those already initiated into the Christian mysteries and lore. Although she does not stray from orthodoxy, Proba takes great liberty to make poetic expansions on the basic bones of the stories so that the point of the story is often lost. Perhaps this lack of pertinent detail to flesh out the theological interests of the stories, and the general obscurity of the text were reasons why Gelasius felt uneasy with the Cento and placed it among apocryphal literature.

Other difficulties with the text arise from the fact that Proba lacks the specific Christian names of Jesus, Mary and the like since Vergil had never employed such terms. She is forced to use general and vague words such as mater, dominus deus, pater, magister, vates to designate these princjpal personages. Necessary passives and circumlocutions brought about by the same absences in Vergil of appropriate terminology render the text impassible at times.

Several words undergo an interesting reinterpretation with her use of them in a Christian context. Light (e.g. at 1. 206) becomes knowledge, usually saving knowledge or revelation. Secreta, which originally meant hidden recesses, becomes the term for divine mysteries, the hiddenness, the unattainable nature or God (1. 464). Tantae pietatis imago originally referred to the Sibyl but is used by Proba to refer to Adam (1. 118). Perhaps the most interesting is her

39

description of the snake which tempts Eve to sin, tyrannus: a tyrant who binds the souls of people. Her usage parallels Jesus' references to Satan as the "strong one" who "binds" the human.

Most of the time Proba transfers the verses from Vergil to analogous contexts in the cento. This makes for the smoothest passages in the poem, the idyllic life of Adam and Eve, the slaughter of the innocents, and the storm on the lake. Sometimes, however, the borrowings, complete in themselves, come from odd sections of Vergil. The verses used of the creation of Eve, for example, come from the boxing match in Aeneid V. 378f.

Among the more fascinating features of the cento are the lines with sudden shifts in tense (ll. 253, 261, 377, 379, 409, inter al.). This style is reminiscent of Vergil himself and shows how deeply Proba had absorbed the style of her mentor. The translator Manelbaum has written:

The rapid shifts of tense in Vergil, the sudden intrusion of past on present and present on past within the narrative sequence itself...(for which there is) no uniform explanation for these shifts in Vergil; but each instance counts in its place and is motivated there.[10]

This rule can be considered when confronted with the same tendency in Proba.

Prosody is uneven throughout the cento: syllables are lengthened as was the custom of the day, spellings are altered, verbs transposed, and meter abused. Interestingly, however, rhyme, not a feature of poetry of the time, but in its formative stages, appears in 115 lines scattered through-- out the cento; 46 lines of leonine rhyme, and at 1. 657 f. rhyming hexametres.[11]

The cento ends with a six line epilogue, the content of which invites several interpretations. Either Proba is gently admonishing her husband to hold to the faith, or she may be urging him to convert,

Of your grace, my husband, keep this way of worship
Hold this to yourself, my sweet spouse, and if our

Piety deserve, may all our grandsons hold the faith.

From this epilogue one might go against the tradition that this work was written for children and suggest that it was written for her husband, a new convert who like many other educated Romans disliked the clumsy language of Scripture.

Proba's narrative, for all its limitations, is a literal, orthodox, and invaluable educational work. Although she may have been aware of the great controversies which swirled through the fourth century, there is no reflection of them in her work. This is interesting in light of her descendants' protection of the heretic Pelagius several generations later. Her concern was education and the task of what she seemed to consider a simple story simply.

Proba's modern editors have not been kind to her endeavor, whether Aschbach who describes the cento as a "forced adaption in which the naturalness and clarity suffer, or Schenkl who is far more pointed, calling the effort an "absurd attempt to narrate the sacred history in Vergilian verse," and the effect of her use of the grammatical arts, "repellant" or Labriolle who though kinder, calls the Probae Cento "a chimerical undertaking, the difficulties of which no device could surmount."

In Metaphor and Reality Philip Wheelwright speaks of "tensive" symbols, that is, symbols with roots in the past which draw on those roots for meaning as well as evoke new associations in new context.[12] While it may be true that Vergil might be surprised at Proba's use of his images, and even mourn for the structure of his poetry, the use she makes of them is attractive from a Christian viewpoint. While the Roman images of Vergil "color the Biblical report" they do so only in the sense that they enliven it, not distort it. Interestingly, in their new contexts, the old images are not distorted either but reveal new dimensions of their meanings.

In the passages describing the creation, for instance, Proba uses many lines from Aeneid I in which Jupiter reveals the future. He is pictured as the "majestic master of the world enthroned above suffering and passion."[13] This serene God, who has foreknowledge arranges and restrains the natural forces and calls humans to their destiny is not unlike the God-creator of Genesis I. In this portion Proba has

41

used the lines of Vergil's _Aeneid_ to speak of this creator
by paraphrase: "the one who turns all things over in his
mind," "the divine goodness," and the "all-knowing god."
None of these images strays from the orthodox formularies
of her time.

In Vergil the demonic is rife, in the soul as passion,
and in the state as civil war.[14] Proba begins her cento with
a reference to civil war as if to remind us of our human condition and its history. She goes on to narrate the salvation
of humanity. Surely in thus structuring her cento, Proba is
true to both the progress of the Biblical epic as well as to
the Vergilian epic, strife to salvation, disorder to order,
chaos to ordained purpose.

A fuller comparison of the cento with the _Aeneid_,
Eclogues, and _Georgics_ might reveal parallels in the understanding of sin as fleeing our created self and its rooted-
ness in the divine. Comparisons between Aeneas and Jesus
might point up the understanding of the saviour as the one
who transcends the past, and by suffering and self-searching,
orients self to transform the future.[15]

The success of Proba's cento as a school text has already been noted. In this fact alone lies the strength of
her credentials as a lay woman who wrote a theological work
and served as a teacher. Her place as an artist of Latin
literature is less secure as her work leaves much to be
desired in the matter of style. One must agree, however,
with the assessment of Isidore of Seville, "if we do not
admire her conception, we admire her ingenuity."

NOTES

1. Joseph Ritter von Aschbach, _Die Anicier und die Romische Dichterin Proba_ (Wien: n.p., 1870).

2. _Poetae Christiani: Minores, Pars I: Probae Cento_, ed. Carol Schenkl, in _CSEL_ (Vienna: n.p., 1890).

3. Pierre de Labriolle, _The History and Literature of Christianity_, (New York: Barnes and Noble, Inc., 1966).

4. Joseph Corcopino, _Daily Life in Ancient Rome_, (New Haven: Yale University Press, 1940), p. 85.

5. Elizabeth Schussler-Fiorenza, "Feminist Theology as a Critical Theology of Liberation," _Theological Studies_, 36, No. 4 (December, 1975).

6. Domenico Comparetti, _Virgil in the Middle Ages_, (Hatden: Archon Books, 1966), pp. 46-54.

7. Labriolle, p. 321.

8. Tertullian, "De Praescriptione Haereticorum", Chapter 39.

9. On the other hand Avitus may have been influenced by the form of the Salvation story commonly memorized in the catechuminate and memorialized in St. Augustine's _De Catechizandis Rudibus_.

10. Allen Mandelbaum, "Introduction," _The Aeneid of Virgil_, (New York: Bantam, 1972), p. x.

11. Maimilianus Maintius, _Geschichte der Christlichlatinischen Poesie_, (Stuttgart: n.p., 1891), pp. 127-128.

12. Philip Wheelwright, _Metaphor and Reality_, (Bloomington: Indiana University Press, 1962), p. 46.

13. Victor Poechl. "Basic Themes", in _Virgil_, ed. Steele Commager (Englewood Cliffs: Prentice-Hall, Inc., 1966), p. 167.

14. _Ibid._, p. 168.

15. Commager, *op. cit.*, pp. 6-13.

PROBA'S CENTO

Of old, I confess, I wrote of chiefs who violated holy
   covenants of peace,
of chiefs whom the fell lust for power made miserable,
   of mutual slaughter, of king's cruel wars and kindred
   battlelines, of glorious chiefs soiled with parents' blood,
5
of trophies not taken from an enemy,
   of bloody triumphs which fame relates and of cities
so many times deprived of their numberless citizens.
Enough to call to mind these woes!
Now, almighty God, I pray, receive this holy song
10
and unloose the lips of your everlasting, sevenfold spirit
and open the inner-most sanctuaries of my heart
so that I, Proba the seer, may reveal all the sacred
   mysteries.
It is not now my concern to seek the ambrosial nectar for
   myself
nor my delight to lead the muses down from the Aonian peak;
15
   let not vain error persuade me to tell of rocks
or seek tripods laureled though they be
or empty prayers or the quarreling gods of rulers or conquered penates.
For it is not task to extend fame with words
   and search into glory, small as it is, with human pursuits.
20
But dripping from the Castalian font and in imitation of the
   saints,
I shall begin now to hymn the libations of holy light
which in my thirst I have drunk. Be present, O God, and
   guide my mind.
May I tell how Vergil sang of Christ's holy gifts.
I shall make this story clear to all, commencing at the
   very beginning,
25
if there is any faith in my soul, in true understanding,
   infused through my limbs, shapes the mass and inspiration
   pervades my body
and to the extent that harmful bodies do not clog
   nor earthly limbs and members moribund deaden.
O Father, O everlasting power over humans and universe,

45

30
grant me smooth sailing and come into my heart,
draw near and accompany me on the difficult journey I have
    undertaken.
O Son, your might and origin is from your almighty heavenly
    father
whom we were first to revere and whose due worship we renew,
Offspring ever young whom every age believed in.
35
For I remember as I ponder the monuments of people of old
that Musaeus, your poet, before all others, sang throughout
    the world
what things are, what were, what things it is said will
    happen soon.
All these things the tender orb of the earth itself caused
    to grow.
O Blessed is the one who could understand the causes of the
    universe,
40
whence the races of humans and of beasts and the life of
    flying things
and what wonders the sea bears beneath its glassy surface
and likewise the streaming fires and heaven's fitful vapors.
I should believe that at the very birth of the infant world
days grew light in this way; such was their course.
45
For me a greater order has been brought to the universe
if thoughts of eternity can bring faith in such a great
    event.
For, Yes, I confess, I used to sing of trivial spectacles;
always I sang of horses and arms, of heroes and battles.
With zeal for vain labor did I ply my craft.
50
As I tried everything a greater will seemed
to reveal truths buried deep in earth and fog.
Day after day my mind stirred, eager to try
something great, content with neither peace nor rest.
Be silent all, be attentive and joyful,
55
mothers, fathers, boys and unwed girls.
First heaven and earth and the expanses of sea
and the shining orb of the moon and the laboring sun
did the Father himself establish. Then you, O most bright
    luminaries of the world
who lead through heaven the gliding years.

46

60
For the fires of the stars did not exist nor did the bright
   ether.
But black night, carried aloft by his chariot, held sway
   over the sky
and chaos plunged headlong into the gloom
as far as one's skyward gaze could see into etherial
   Olympus.
Then the almighty Father, whose sway over the universe is
   supreme
65
removed the darksome air and dispelled the shades
and divided the world into two, giving half to light and
   half to night. [Gen.1.4.
                    Gen. 1.16.]
All the stars gliding in the silent sky He observed
turning his attentive eyes here and there to see
where he should direct the heat of the south wind,
what rearward parts he should turn towards the north pole.
70
When the almighty saw that all stood right in the serene sky
He numbered and named the stars
and He made the year equal to four varied seasons [Gen.1.14]
with their warm spells, rains and cold-bearing winds.
And this He did that we might learn from unfailing signs
75
how in spring the Earth swells and calls for life-giving
   seeds
and in the heat of mid-summer the threshing floor grinds the
   parched ears;
then autumn causes her various fruits to fall
and dark winter comes; Sicyon's olives are crushed in the
   press
and the year rolls back upon itself, retracting its steps.
80
Now from that time mighty heaven
uniting with earth's great body nourishes her offspring with
   fertile rains.
And now for the first time Dawn sprinkled the earth with her
   new born rays of light
and ushered in the day when the stars had fled.
Then He begins to firm up the soil and to confine Nereus to
   his sea
85
and little by little to assign forms to things.

47

Amidst the manifold shapes of the sea, the monstrous whales
swept the seas with their tails and cleft the surge.
Also the watery species of the vast deep,
now that the world was suffused with sun and revealed by the
     light of day,
90
froliced scattering far and wide the briny spray.
And now the second day was rising with the earliest morning
     star.
The earth poured forth flowers unfolding all her foliage
     [Gen.1.11]
and the wild haunts of birds blush with blood-red berries;
not subject they to hoes or other human care.
95
The third day had removed from heaven the cool shade.
Then the distant thickets resounded with melodious birds
     [Gen.1.22]
and ravens with narrowed throats send forth their liquid
     songs;
nor did the turtledove cease cooing from its airy elm.
On the fourth day the earth suddenly brought forth the
     forests [Gen.1.24]
100
marvellous varieties of beasts and flocks of every kind
untended on the grass--a wondrous thing to behold.
Then finally the lion woke for battle; then the fell tiger,
the scaly serpent and the lioness of tawny neck
grew fierce and the shapes of giant wolves howled.
105
Other herds grazed on green herbs;
flocks lacked neither clear waters nor pastures.
Days pass and all this work of His righteousness,
this share of the divine mind, the Creator
surveyed. The world was completed on time
110
and He could not state His mind, but as He looked He thrilled
     [Gen.1.25]
at the lands, the tracts of sea and heaven profound.
The races of flying things and the flocks, they, He decided,
should hold sway over the sea and the land, [Gen.1.26]
and fields would not lie fallow. Ever it pleased Him to
     take His time.
115
Of a sudden, as He pondered, His will took shape:
Rich clay He took up and shaped it,

48

molding fertile earth from the first months of the year.
And now, unexpectedly, the novel form of a man came forth,
the likeness of His great holiness, beautiful beyond all else,
120
like unto God in face and body, whose mind and soul
God in His greatness directs and moves towards deeds of
   moment.
Now another is sought for this one; but none dares come forth
to be called his comrade in sovereignty.
Without delay God brings restful slumber
125
to the young man's limbs; his eyes sink into blissful sleep.
And in the midst of dark night's course,
The Almighty Creator lays bare his ribs and entrails.
He ripped one of the ribs from the well-formed sides of the
   man
and from it is born a wondrous gift---
130
it is a marvellous story---a maiden shone forth
in brightest light, beautiful of face and breast
already ripe for husband, in age right for marriage.
Now his sleep is broken by fear unbounded; bones and limbs
summon him to marriage and dazed by divinity
135
he embraced her, took her hand, and clung to her in love.
   [Gen.2.24]
These things at length having been accomplished, He who turns
   the world's stars
begins; as he speaks the sea calms its waters
and earth is shaken to her base; the lofty heaven grows
   silent.
"Live happily amond the radiant crops [Gen.1.28]
140
and the blessed seats of blissful groves. [Gen.2.15]
This is your home, this is your fatherland; here is sure rest
   from your toils.
I place neither bounds nor limits on your kingdom.
I have given you an everlasting empire and for many years
   the earth
shall not feel the hoe nor the vine the pruning-knife.
145
The race remains immortal and old age that slows
does not weaken the minds; strength nor alter its vigor.
But pay attention to what I am about to say.
There is in sight a tree with glorious branches,

which it is forbidden to all to lay low with fire or tool.
150
Divine law decrees that it never be disturbed.
Whosoever shall pluck the sacred fruit from this holy tree
shall die deservedly. I shall not change my mind.
And let no adviser seem so wise as to persuade you
to soil your hands -- my voice should be a warning to you --
155
lady, and let no one's force prevail over you,
if the glory of this divine land is to remain worthy of you.
Afterwards the Father whom the stars obey
put all things in order and passed laws, and from above
Showed off the gleaming plains, glory of the vast universe.
160
But behold, hard upon the rising sun's first light
they came to a place where soft marjoram
embraced them with blossoms and sweet shade.
Here is rosy spring, and summer in other months,
here clear fountains, here honey swells [Gen.2.6,10]
165
in seasons appointed by heaven. Here white poplar shades a
     cave
and gentle vines weave round shady nooks.
Gardens redolent with crocuses invite them in
amidst groves perfumed by laurels, and the earth itself
brought forth all things gladly though no one bade.
170
Blessed pair---if only the mind of the sinful wife
had not been perverse! Too late the dreadful event taught
     her.
And now the dreadful day was at hand; behold through the
     flowery fields [Gen.3.1]
the enemy -- a snake (atrocious) with immense coils,
seven huge spirals, seven folds writhing
175
not an easy thing to look at nor easy for anyone to describe,
with bitter envy it hung from a leafy bough,
panting its viperous breath, its heart set on dreadful
     struggles,
wrath, treachery and heinous crimes.
Even God the Father despised it.
180
It bristles with scales erect and lest it should leave some
     crime
or deceit undared, untried, it first accosted her

50

with words and freely presented itself to view:
"Tell me, O Maiden -- we dwell in shady groves
and we make our beds on river banks and in the meadows kept
  moist by streams --
185
why has so much cowardice come into your hearts?
Strewn everywhere beneath the trees lie the fruits of each;
Your cups are liquid springs; yet it is a sin to touch
  heavene's gifts;
that one thing you lack.
Bur what prevents you from testing thoroughly the hidden
  causes?
190
It is vain superstition. One half of your world is missing.
For what purpose did He give you life eternal? Why has he?
If you do not deem my words idle,
I shall give you the courage to relax the sacred laws.
You are his wife; it is permissible for you to test his mind
  by entreaty.
195
I shall be your leader; if I can be sure of your good will,
then we shall build couches and dine on sumptuous foods."
Thus he spoke and quicker than a word, what was probhibited
  by law,
the once venerated fruit of the tree they feasted on
and spread a banquet and by their touch they defiled all
  things.
200
And Eve, ill starred beyond all and doomed to impending
  disaster, [Gen.3.6]
admired the fresh leaves and the fruit not meant to be hers,
the cause of so much evil she touched to her lips.
Then initiating a still greater sin and loosing greater
  madness,
alas, to her poor husband she offered the fruit of Another's
  tree,
205
and won immediate consent with her sweetness.
Straight way a strange light dazzled their eyes; they,
  [Gen.3.7]
terrified by the unexpected sight, tarrying no longer,
hid their bodies behind branches with leafy cover,
a garment fashioned for themselves, and no hope of aid was
  offered them.

210

But the creator of humanity and world
does not watch with unseeing eyes; He saw the crime, the
    deed of a despot;
what a mad woman could do was known to him.
At once He accosted them, "Away, away O unclean ones,"
He shouts who guides heaven and earth with his nod.

215

But they, when they note him striding along in deadly rage,
they turn in fear and flee
stealthily seeking the woods and rocky hollows wherever.
They loathe what they have done and the light of day
which they cannot bear to look at; they are weary of gazing
    at heaven's vault.

220

Before much time had elapsed, crowding their ears,
there seemed to be the sound of feet, and the Father
addressed him; where he discerned his sorrowful form amidst
    the shade,
and with words such as these He rebuked him:
"Unhappy man, how could such madness have seized your mind?

225

What kind of strange aberration is this of yours? Whither
    now, whither are you heading?
unmindful of your kingdom? What is this insanity that has
    warped your mind?
Tell me, what is this mad longing for light that you poor
    wretches have?
Flee -- be gone from this whole grove
and do not come back even if adversity summons you.

230

It is not permitted; a river with torrents of flames surrounds
    it
and roars through the middle, and churns up resounding rocks
and balls of fire and it licks the stars."
To this Adam said, "Your angry face, O Father... [Gen.3.12]
have placed us in this place. I deserve punishment and I do
    not ask for mercy.

235

Almighty, I tremble at the sound of your feet and at your
    voice
aware of our audacity; inspite of dire warnings,
a woman brought tart juices and a lingering flavor.
She, pondering treachery and monstrous crime in her heart,
a maid, doomed to die a frenzied death, has brought

52

240
a cruel death to me an innocent though careless man.
She persuaded me as you yourself know, for it is not possible
    to deceive you.
When I beheld it, when I brought ruin to myself, when wicked
    sin carried me off,
we picked with our hands fruit not produced by the tree it
    was on."
Then the Almighty Father said from his throne on high:
    [Gen.3.14]
245
"Take, therefore, these words of mine to heart and fix them
    there:
You, first of all, more monstrous at crime than all others,
whom neither passage of time nor piety softens,
instigator of sin, O serpent, who feel on evil grasses,
a drag ignobly a paunch broad from slothfulness,
250
get thee from this place -- no man restrains you --
to a place where clay is scarce and there is gravel in
    thorny fields."
Then he exclaimed, "But all your life because of your crime,
    your audacity
you shall be worn out by use of iron tools,
and, O pitiable man, alas, you will be the first to scrape
    the earth with hoe
255
and frighten away birds with your voice; the thistle shall
    flourish
in your field along with sharp thorns
and burs and caltrops and the false poison-plant.
And if for a harvest of wheat or of hardy spelt
you ply the soil, in vain shall you look for abundance;
260
and in the woods, rather, shall you try to satisfy your
    hunger, shaking the oak for acorns.
Moreover, disease shall steal in and gloomy old age
and suffering and death, harsh and merciless, shall carry
    you off.
This will always be your lot. And you, cruelest of wives,
    [Gen.3.16]
Who are acquainted with evil, the cause and origin of these
    woes,
265
you launched corruption into the world. Alas, lost one,

53

you know not, neither can you see what perils shall henceforth
  surround you.
Now you shall die deservedly; this is what you sought with
  your whole mind.
My decision will not be altered nor will it give way."
At first a cruel terror seized the young man.
270
His eyes became fixed, and he could no longer hide himself
  in the shadows;
he could not understand or utter words.
Tarrying not, they hastened on as bidden, moving with swift
  step [Gen.3.23]
and side-by-side they went through the dark paths
choosing a middle course. They crossed the threshold
275
weeping, sharing their anxiety.
They found sustenance in the woods; berries and hard cornel-
  cherries
branches provided. Herbs and roots nourished them.
Meanwhile the sun rolls round the year's mighty cycle.
Ten months brought the mother prolonged travail;
280
from her sons were born, a hardy race. Thence through skill
they made herbs grow in fields and foliage on trees.
Grasses boldly trusted themselves to fresh sunlight.
They began to cultivate grapes on slow-growing vines
and taught them to cling to moist bark.
285
Then while altars reeked of pine-wood, the twin brothers
grew jealous, one of the other, jealous of sacrifices
  offered---
with shudders I report this---one caught his nearest of kin
unawares and cut him down at the altar of their fathers,
polluting with blood fires he himself had sanctified.
290
Then it was that the Creator instilled venom into fell
  serpents,
shook honey from trees, took fire away,
made wolves plunder and oceans swell,
and stopped the winds.
Soon also plague fell on the corn, a pestilential mildew
295
gnawed at the stalks; dying crops denied them sustenance.
Then men discovered how to catch wild beasts with traps and
  trick birds

with bird-lime, and in those evil days growing poverty
afflicted the land, anxiety sharpened mortal wits,
till little by little an age of decline, a tarnished time
   crept in. [Gen. 6.4]
300
A race of iron reared its head from the harsh fields.
There followed a madness for war and a craving for
   possessions.
Justice withdrew, leaving only her footprints on earth.
Only a short period intervened, fury and wrath
dethroned reason. Soaked with brothers' blood men rejoiced.
305
One hoards wealth and brooks over buried gold,
no sympathy for the poor, never a helping-hand.
Then the Father Almighty, sore concerned, descended
   [Gen. 6.5 sq.]
from heaven high and mingling all in deluge,
He plunged land into water, merging heaven and hell.
   [Gen. 7.17]
310
Then fields are laid low and flourishing crops; the work
   of oxen
washed away. Ravines are filled; rivers rise in their beds.
Every kind of beast--tame or wild--it carried off to death.
Then a man, venerated for his holiness and good deeds--it
   is wonderful to report this--
the man most observant of justice of all who were then on
   earth,
315
God rescued from death, from the surging waves,
that He might have whence to produce a new race.
From the time of the flood the Almighty gave laws
to the elders assembled; under the majesty of the law they
   began to live.
Why should I recall heinous crimes, why the deeds of tyrants,
320
and hearts unmoved by human prayers,
and why the might of Egypt and the East and distant wars,
or magnanimous leaders chosen from the ranks of whole
   peoples,
or how the desert was sought by tribes and families
of heroes great, ever mindul of their worth?
325
Or why tell which priests were chaste behind their altars
or which seers fell in piety for freedom's sake,

which kings were driven to was, what battle lines
filled fields by strands red with blood, with what weapons
a king enraged a race renowned as fury flamed
330
and led their cavalry and troops resplendent with bronze?
The other deeds of our fathers, the wars fought one after
   another
I omit and leave the telling of them to others after me.
Now to Thee, O Father and to Thy great plans I return.
A greater task I must commence. The prophecies of old seers
335
I approach, though a short life-span limits me,
the way must be tried whereby I can raise
myself up from the ground and gain renown that will endure
   forever,
because Thy Son descended from high heaven
and time brought to us with our hopes at last
340
succour and the coming of God whom for the first time a
   woman
bearing the guises and habit of a virgin--marvelous to say--
brought forth, a child not of our race or blood
and in manner terrifying prophets sang of omens to come:
a man would come to earth and its peoples, raised on high
345
by heaven's seed and who would possess the earth in might.
And now the promised day was at hand when first
He showed His hallowed face, the first of a holy race
sent for a kingdom, and virtue came in his body
one with God, the very image of His beloved Sire.
350
And without delay in heaven's peaceful quarter
a star, brilliant and leaving a trail appeared.
The leaders recognized divinity and forthwith collected
gifts for the sacred star and honored it.
Then indeed their faith was made manifest and the name of
   His paternal
355
strength was glorified; they recognized His countenance
and the tokens of the divine glory of the radiant God.
Straightway the news is brought to the king of fervent men,
   fleet to foot.
His wrath waxed at the reports,
and his soul was inflamed. The news reaches His mother's
   ears.

360
She, acquainted with the world's ways, sensed treachery
    and dreadful sins;
she was the first to suspect what was to come.
With prescience she ordered the child to be reared in hiding,
while the king's intentions were unclear and his mind
    seethed with anger.
But the king, greatly disturbed, decreed that the child and
    all its future race
365
be cast down or consumed by flames. [Matth. 2.16]
The movement gathers momentum and he orders men sent to
    bring back
reports unambiguous. They do as told and proceed
    double-time
and fill the city with terror and fear.
Immediately wailing is heard, the screams
370
of weeping children. Before the faces of their parents,
the bodies of the children are laid on the threshold.
But His mother, not vainly terrified by such suffering,
    [Matth. 2. 13-14]
bearing before her the Babe, fled from the tumult and
    returned to the manger rich.
375
Here beneath the roof of the humble shed
she nursed with her breasts His tender lips.
Here, O child, your abode first brought forth flowers
    for you
and the earth everywhere is sprinkled with smiling foxglove
and little by little the Egyptian lily will mingle with
    the soft acanthus.
380
And now an end came, time's cycle was completed.
As soon as the furor subsided and the rabid tongues grew
    silent,
bearing character precocious, Heaven's first born
strode through the midst of cities and neighboring peoples.
Him all the young, streaming from house and field,
385
gaping with minds thunder-struck, watched as he passed.
Crowds cf matrons marveled, "The Spirit is upon Him;
what a countenance He has! What a voice, and the gait, as
    he passes!"

At once a prophet, a most reliable witness,
when he espied a secluded spot far off by a cool stream,
  cried,
390
"It is the Lord's time. Behold the Lord, to Him belongs
  the greatest faith
in world or word. Thou now shalt be the Vicar,
O blessed Son, of Him whom the stars obey.
Thus indeed I wondered in my mind and contemplated the
  future;
Thou are come, O long awaited one, our hope and our comfort."
395
When he had uttered these words, the prophet
received Him into the waters of salvation and baptized Him
  with gentle waters:
The rivers rejoiced and suddenly a dove, inspired,
flew down and hesitated over His hear; then she skims
the liquid air, moving not her swift wings.
400
Hither ran the whole crowd, rushing to the banks [Mark 1.5]
vying with one another to pour the abundant waters over their
  shoulders.
Then the Father addressed His Son with loving words:
  [Mark 1.11]
"My Son, you alone are my strength, my might power;
you are about to bring sweet glory to your Sire,
405
All things begin and end with you. Accept, I implore,
O my son, both oceans which the sun surveys
in its rounds. Once your task is completed,
in joy you shall behold all things revolving beneath your
  feet.
Rule your people with authority, both men and women.
410
Already you calm their pride and their hearts grown cold,
And with me you have compassion for slothful humans, those
  ignorant of the way.
Go forth and become used to being invoked with prayers."
God had spoken. He prepared to obey the commands
of his Almighty Father, eager for his task and the kingdom
  to come.
415
Alas for holiness, alas for old-time faith! What thanks
shall I commence to offer, if it is permissible to return
  a pittance for such great things?

58

For me there was no longer hope of seeing the ancient
   fatherland,
no hope for freedom, no concern for salvation.
He was the first to give answer to my petition;
420
he removed the inborn stain and left a pure,
spiritual sensation, and He sent me back to my realms.
I would follow Him through flames were I an exile in Africa,
through misfortunes of all sorts, though a thousand missiles
   come at me,
withersoever situations tended, Him alone, because of his
   great name,
425
I would follow, and I would strew His altars with gifts.
At His coming, in honor of such great praises,
the mountains and their woods raise their voices
to the stars in joy. The valleys echo it all.
At this time, one perforce recalls--a great and memorable
430
name---the frenzied curse of the serpent.
It even dared---though the story grows dim with time---
dared to accost the Man and demand His reasons for coming.
For when it espied Him approaching through the grass,
the serpent halted, hissed ferociously and in hurt and
   haughty
435
tones addressed its all-powerful master:
"Is this your true face? Do you come to me as a true
   messenger?
What is your race? Where is your home, O you who have come
   to our home?
Come now tell me, why are you come? They say that you give
   laws.
Who, O most confident of youth, bid you draw near our house
440
and make a habit of peace?
Indeed I do not envy you; rather I marvel. Learn now
why I doubt and what thoughts come to my mind.
There is a lofty house: summon the winds and glide on wings
to the high roof, dare to trust yourself to heaven
445
to see if now the Father whom you speak of exists, he whom
   the stars obey."
Smiling he spoke with tranquil heart
not ignorant of the prophets, nor the age to come.

"Did you expect to fool me, you lying serpent?
Do not hesitate, for you know the truth. Seek the stars on
   high,
450
if you wish, or close yourself up in the hollow earth.
Whither do you rush, you who are about to die and why do you
attempt things beyond your strength? Give in to God and
   fling
your whole body on the ground." He said no more than this;
   it awed
by the vernerable gift, pressed its head to the ground and
   spewed bloody foam from its mouth,
455
and content to flee it hid itself amidst the shade.
Meanwhile fame flies through the great cities.
To all there is one intention, to follow
to whatever lands he should wish to lead them by sea.
Many also whom obscure fame hid
460
come together noisily and crowd around in throngs,
and rejoice in their hearts; for a vast throng
holds him in the middle and looks up as he towers over them
   on high.
After he had reached the hills, His eternal power
granted rights and laws for men, His Father's secrets,
465
and He gave hope to minds in doubt and banished cares.
And behold He caught sight of others crowding in on left
   and right.
When He saw that they were eager to fight, [Matth. 5.1sq.]
He began and inspired diving love with His words:
"Learn justice, ye who have been warned, bring aid to the
   weary,
470
each for his own sake, and, my friends, whenever there is an
   opportunity
invoke your common God. Let us pursue what is best
and let us turn wither the path summons. First of all
inviolate faith is the way to salvation and a mind conscious
   of what is right.
When the cycle of time is completed, ye shall have peace.
475
For those who in solitude devoted themselves to wealth that
   they had won
and did not set aside a portion for their heirs, while

alive,
or struck a parent or defrauded a client,
when chill death has separated body and soul,
in bondage shall they await their punishment (and their
  number is very large).
480
The punishment they summon from infernal darkness, and they
  shall pay
the penalty for their ancient wrongs, Some have the stain
  of sin
washed out by swirling floods or burned out by fire.
Here turbid with muck a whirlpool of abysmal depth
seethes and belches sand from the bottom of the pit.
485
From there groans can be heard and the cruel sound
of the whip, next the clang of iron and the dragging of
  chains,
and darkness ever thickening beneath night's gloom.
Further, heed with your hearts what I say.
In the future let me not hear that you are honoring
490
statues and temples made by mortal hand of tree trunks
with bulls duly slain as was your fathers' wont.
For repeating these warnings I shall time and time admonish
  you.
To die once is enough, but if your faith is worthy,
it will benefit you to be mindful of both Son and Father.
495
But times flies; it flies and cannot be recalled,
  [Matth. 24.29 sq.]
and the day of flames draws near and the forces of the
  enemy." [Mark 13.24 sq.]
Amazed in their hearts, they stood; and without delay he
  pronounced [Luke 21.25 sq.]
another and greater judgment on poor, suffering
humankind--and he threatened dreadful wrath.
500
All is coming to destruction, all things convulsed in
  ruinous devastation
and the stars that roam in the firmament shall mingle
in raging flames and heaven itself collapse.
Then indeed fresh fears crept into the terrified hearts of
  all
and silence they saw what was coming.

61

505
As He was warning of coming horrors, [Matth. 19.16 sq.]
a young man, his face showing the first down of youth,
  [Mark 10.17 sq.]
rich and flush with zeal of shameless leisure---
  [Luke 18.18 sq.]
he owned five bleating flocks; five herds
returned from pasture and piled his table high for feasts
  gratis.
510
Suddenly he stretched both palms forth eagerly
and clasping His knees, he spoke with loving words:
"O Glorious One, to Thee rightly belongs the greatest share
  of our renown.
To Thee I flee and as a suppliant I beseech Thy godhead.
I have reviewed all things in my soul; all things I have
  anticipated.
515
Rescue me now from these woes, Unconquerable One. What
  now remains for me?
By what course could I survive such great suffering?
Accept and return my pledge; it is right for me to carry
  out Thy commands."
The Hero responded thus briefly:
"Young man of noble soul, cease beseeching me,
520
and be not sorry, my friend; you have left nothing undone.
I shall even add this: if your good will is certain,
learn, my child, to despise wealth and make yourself
  worthy of God,
then you shall learn what virtue is.
Lend a hand to the poor and let not brother forsake brother.
525
If anyone of good will is eager to join in friendship, join
  him,
Let your home be chaste and let it preserve its modesty.
Come now, delay not and be not disdainful of poverty."
This He spoke, and as He spoke the young man turned
away sad, holding up his face noticeably pale.
530
Avoiding his eyes, he departed lamenting much.
From that time when people first entrusted themselves to
  the sea [Mark 6.48 sq.]
and comrades pulled ships to the tranquil deep, one with
  exquisite skill [Matth. 14.22 sq.]

lashes broad waters with casting-net
seeking the depths while another trolls the sea with damp
     line.
535
After their ships gained the deep and lands
were no longer visible, the heavens lighted constantly with
     fiery flashes;
suddenly clouds carried off the sky and the day,
the winds arose and raised waves toward the stars.
The comrades' blood chilled and froze with sudden fear;
540
their spirits sank and all in tears
regarded the sea---in unison they cried.
Hesitating between hope and fear, not knowing
whether they should plan to live or suffer the ultimate.
     They were within
a hair's breadth of death, but such are the perils people
     suffer on the high seas.
545
But lo! God knew that the sea was churning with mighty roar
and that a storm had been let loose, God whose power is
     supreme.
Light as the wind and swifter than a lightning bolt
He sought the up-turned waters and moved across the open sea.
He took a stand not far from the sailing ship.
550
The naked crew recognized from afar their King, His strong
     right hand,
and they hailed Him with loud cries.
After He touched the towering waves and came to calm waters,
this awesome and miraculous sight was reported:
The waves subsided so that to row was no longer a struggle.
555
He disperses the gathered clouds and strides through the
     expanse
yet no wave moistened His towering flanks.
But stepping aboard at midship among the crew,
the Pilot himself, the Master took the helm.
The mast quivered, the bark groaned beneath His bulk.
560
The sails collapsed as God took His seat on the high deck.
At length rejoicing they were born towards familiar shores.
Later He sat as a rider upon the back of a slow-moving
     donkey,

radiant as a cloud. For Him mothers,
fathers and children lay down many a treasured cloak
565
and they rejoice to touch the halter with their hands.
And now they approach the gates, and He enters the venerable
    temple
with its one hundred lofty columns of ancient cedar,
surrounded by a vast throng.
This temple, awesome amidst the grove, was their senate.
570
This was their sacred seat, and they cherished it with
    marvelous rites.
Now while he surveyed the great edifice's features one by
    one,
He suddenly shuddered at the sight; He cracked a whip
    [Matth. 21.12]
And waved His hand as He roared in mighty voice:
    [Mark 11.15 sq.]
"What kinds of sin do I see? Why do I see bronze flashing
    [Luke 19.45 sq.]
575
and even Caesar's name? Has madness infected your minds?
These sites belong to Us. Here at appointed times
it has been our custom to take our seats at the ever-
    enduring tables of our fathers."
Their minds were struck dumb, and a chilly tremor ran
through the very marrow of their bones; fearfully the
    leaders left the tables.
580
Meanwhile from Olympus' slope evening drew nearer.
    [Matt. 26.20]
Then men restored their strength with food and reclining
    on the grass [Mark 14.17 sq.]
they piled the tables high with vituals and passed the cup.
    [Luke 22.14 sq.]
Afterwards rest came, the tables were removed,
and He Himself was among the first to honor the Father.
585
looking toward heaven. Tongues grew silent.
He gives with His hands fruit, and sweet water from a font,
and He filled a bowl with wine, and He taught them
the rite of the celebration. Then amidst prayers He said,
"Hear me, ye leaders of the people, learn what is your hope.
590
No one of this number will depart without a reward from Me.

64

Because of My Father's promises, your rewards remain certain,
My children, and no one alters the prize because of rank.
As soon as tomorrow's dawn returns to earth,
one only from our group will there be against Me,
595
bent on destruction of My followers, while he throws
    himself between to sue for peace
And now day is here, if I err not. Banish your cares.
Mine will be the task, and My faith will not fail;
one life shall be given for the many."
Having said this, He grew silent, bring long overdue rest
    to His limbs.
600
Meanwhile Dawn rising left behind the ocean
and now the priests fill the regions far and wide with their
    laments
together with the people and the elders; A murmur passes
    through their ranks.
What race of men is this? What country so barbarous
that it would allow this? Coming together they demand
605
punishment with blood and they follow the innocent man with
    much shouting.
The hearts of the ignoble rabble grow fierce.
The fiery sun had risen to the zenith of the sky
when suddenly all the people and leaders
demand that He be summoned to tell from what family He came,
610
what He wants or what He has to say.
Grief mingled with astonishment urges the dolts on as they
    behold His glorious deeds.
O ignorant mortal mind! They vie with one another to taunt
    the captive, [Matth. 26.27; 27.29]
taking up weapons, they converge from all sides. Clamor
    rises to the sky [Mark 15.19]
and suddenly all seize the sacred effigy; with bloody hands
615
they raise the huge tree, its branches pruned
and they bind Him with mighty ropes.
His hands they stretched out; His feet fastened one to the
    other--- [Luke 23.33]
a sad task---and they whom the young followed
620
dared with success to commit a monstrous sin.

65

He, however, spoke without fear, "Why fetter me?
Do you have so much faith in your own kind?
You will pay for what you've done with penalty of a
   different sort."
He continued to remind them of such things though He
   remained fixed.
625
Meanwhile the sky darkened with a might roar
and black night took away colors from the world
and the unholy age feared eternal night.
The earth quaked, wild beasts fled and mortal hearts
were laid low by abject terror, nation by nation.
630
Then suddenly the earth gave forth a groan; the sky
   resounded with thunder.
Immediately bodiless shades, disturbed, came up from deepest
   hell.
The earth also and the expanses of the sea
bore witness; rivers stood still and the earth split open.
Yes, the very mansions of hell and innermost Tartarus were
   struck dumb
635
and their shadowy caverns lay open on all sides.
The sun also, although it was rising--all say they know---
then hid its radiant face with darksome haze.
Companions scattered and are swallowed up by black night,
and sad in heart they wondered at the harshness of their lot.
640
What should they do? His face and words clung fixed in
   their breasts,
but anxiety does not allow peaceful rest to their members.
Then an elder, pondering much in his heart, spoke thus:
"Where now is God, that great Teacher of ours?
Whom shall we follow? Whither do you bid us go? Where is
   our home?
645
O grief and glory, O splendor of these great events!
Now, now there is no delaying; take us with you, come what
   may---
we beg you, do not withdraw from our sight."
In the midst of this commotion, amidst words such as these,
the third day had driven chilly night from heaven,
650
and now day was retracing its steps to the upper air
when suddenly before their eyes the tomb with its great rock

where the lifeless body had been placed---neither bolts nor
guards themselves were strong enough to keep it there---
   they see
the rocks torn from rocks, tight fitting joints loosened.
  [Mark 16.14; Luke 24.2; John 20.1; Matth. 28.2]
655
There is a roar, the earth is shaken by the huge weight.
There was terror in every heart; the very silence was
   horrifying.
But behold from beneath the eaves the first songs of birds;
leaving the tomb He strode, glorious in His victory;
He went forth in triumph, and the earth shrilled, shook with
   the beat of His feet.
660
Bearing those wounds He entered through lofty doors.
And here to His surprise He found that a great number
of disciples had gathered, and without warning [John 20.19]
He spoke, "I whom you seek am here. [Luke 24.33 sq.]
Piety and living virtue have overcome the difficult road."
665
Hasten now, be on guard and let there be no fear.
Behold my return, My longed for triumph.
Behold My great faith. O thrice and four times blessed,
what rewards should I deem worthy for your glorious deeds?
   What gifts?
Take this to heart: the earth which first bore you
670
from your parents' stock, the same will welcome you
with joyful breast. Recall your courage; banish
gloomy fear, and save yourselves for better things.
Be happy with what you have done and
675
pray that peace be at hand. Praise peace, highminded ones,
wherever you are. The pledge of peace is alone inviolable."
And with these words He showed them His face and mouth,
His head, both hands and breast pierced by iron.
They joined hands, rejoicing to gaze at Him.
680
Nor was it enough to see Him once; they took joy in delaying
   Him,
keeping step with Him, and joining hand to hand.
These rites at last completed, He parts the breeze's breath,
and is born through thin air towards the open sky.
He vanished from mortal view in the midst of His teaching,

685
and the palace of starry heaven welcomed Him to His throne,
and holds through the ages His name undying.
From this moment His glory has been celebrated, and posterity
rejoices to observe the day, though so many years have
  glided by since.
Come, Thou who are our glory, glory of the universe,
690
graciously draw near with favoring step to us
and to Thy sacred yearly rites, which only sin would defer.
O friends, cherish and celebrate His sacred traditions,
and Thou, O sweetest spouse, embrace them also, and if our
  devotion
694
merits it, grant that our children remain pure and holy in
  Thy religion.

NOTES

1. Aonian peak = Mt. Helicon in Boeotia on which the Muses dwellt.

2. Castalian font, a celebrated fountain on Mt. Parnassus which was sacred to Apollo and the Muses.

3. Musaeus, a mythical poet, seer and priest who, it was said, lived in pre-Homeric times. He was often associated with Orpheus.

4. Sicyon, an ancient city located in the northeast part of the Peloponnesus (southern Greece) which was famous for the fertility of its soil and consequently for its olives and almonds.

5. Nereus, a sea god, son of Oceanus and Tethys and father of the Nereids, 50 sea nymphs.

INTRODUCTION: THE PILGRIMAGE OF EGERIA

One of the more fascinating documents of the early church was unknown to the modern world until it was discovered in 1884 by G. F. Gamurrini, the Italian historican and archaeologist. Along with some of the works of Hilary of Poitiers, it was found in an eleventh century codex in Arezzo, in the library of the Brotherhood of St. Mary. With the beginning and end of the journal missing, as well as one major lacuna in the middle, Gamurrini published this account of a pilgrimage to various sites in and around the Holy Land, and a lengthy description of the Jerusalem liturgy. Internal evidence indicated to him that it had been written by a woman traveler through Egypt, Palestine, and Syria, probably in the early part of the fifth century. Since then no other copies have been discovered; only a few fragments which add nothing substantive to the text have been found.[1]

Because of the somewhat fragmentary nature of the document, and the absence of contemporary supporting evidence, very little in known about the author of the account. The exact date of the pilgrimage is uncertain, her name is not firmly established, and only inferences can be drawn about her motives, social background, and ecclesial status. Nonetheless, her journal provides us with substantial information about the geography, religious and liturgical life of the church in her time, as well as something about her role and the status of women in her day. Most scholarly attention has been given to her travel journal as a source for liturgical study, geography, and late Latin style and linguistic development, as the bibliographies of secondary works about her travel journal testify. Considerably less paper has been devoted to Egeria's significance in an appraisal of the position of women in this period of the early church, and this introduction will point to some areas which would bear further investigation.

Before proceeding further, it is essential to try to identify what few things that are fairly certain about Egeria. Very little is; almost everything we know about Egeria must be gathered from the internal evidence of the work itself. Even her name is a matter of dispute. Gamurrini called the author "St. Silvia of Aquitaine" and suggested 381-388 as a probable time of composition, basing his identification on a figure known from Palladius' Lausiac History. However, by the beginning of this century Dom Ferotin linked the Perigrinatio Silviae, so named by Gamurrini, to a woman named Aetheria from Galicia in Spain, praised in a letter by a seventh century monk named Valerius. In 1884 Galla Placidia was suggested as the author, and in 1924 an Abbess from Gaul named Flavia was proposed.

Neither of these last two ideas have been accepted, and most people have admitted the usefulness of Ferotin's suggestion. Most of scholarly debate since then has centered in on the issue of what form of Etheria's name was the correct one. Aetheria, Etheria, Echeria, Egeria were all suggested as possible forms, but today the one most preferred is Egeria, and it is that which has been adopted here.[2]

When did Egeria write her account of the pilgrimage? That too is a disputed question. Gamurrini suggested somewhere in the late fourth century, and others have set forth a variety of dates from 363, the earliest possible date of her access as a Roman citizen to some of the sites she mentions, to 540, the latest possible before the Persian destruction of Antioch. Various dates between these two have been proposed since the, and none of them is altogether convincing. Of the most recent translators Gingras suggests a date somewhere between 404-717, Wilkinson between 381-384, each using a different set of data as a basis for dating. The possibilities for trying to determine an exact date could be multiplied. However, Gingras' theory takes account of evidence which Wilkinson's doesn't, and until further archaeological or literary information is uncovered, Gingras' date seems the most preferable.[3]

If both the name and the date of Egeria are in some doubt, can one really know much about her, or are we in the realm of pure conjecture? Pilgrimages were very popular in this period,[4] and Egeria's distinctive contribution is an important one in the genre, which also reveals a great deal about the narrator, Egeria. The very fact that Egeria was on her pilgrimage for several years (she stayed in Jerusalem for three years), a matter of which we are certain from her text, indicates that she must have been of high social status, with considerable money at her disposal.

She travels with an entourage, never indicates any concern
for money to support her either on her travels or during
her stay in Jerusalem, is received by the chief local clergy
and monks, who pray with her and discuss Scripture, and is
escorted by soldiers in dangerous situations. Local clergy
are always eager to show Egeria the sites; the bishop or
presbyter in charge is always happy to explain the virtues
of each place, and to escort her to new ones she may not be
aware of. (e.g., 21.) Perhaps one of the most telling
indicators of Egeria's social status is that she never
questions that this sort of reception is her due, nor is she
surprised. She speaks of her unworthiness for all of these
graces, and her gratitude that God has preserved her to see
all these wonders, and she praises the holiness of those who
received her so hospitably (e.g., 5, 9, 23). She is grate-
ful, but never surprised. Paula, the friend of Jerome, is
received in a similar way according to Jerome's descriptions; she is the wealthy descendant of one of Rome's most
ancient noble families, and even she did not travel as
extensively, for as long a period, or as comfortably as
Egeria. One inference from all the entrees which Egeria's
wealth and standing gave her is that what she saw and
learned enabled her to relate to us the best side of early
fifth century religious observance in the Holy Lands, as
chronicled by a sympathetic and intelligent observer.

Egeria is not a woman learned in the secular classics,
but she is well-read in the Scripture and demonstrates a
thorough grasp of them. We should not be surprised,
because she is clearly a member of a circle of religious
women who made the Scriptures the basis of their learning.
Macrina offers a point of comparison; her brother Gregory
of Nyssa informs us in his Life of Macrina that she was
raised from her youth in a knowledge of Scripture.[5]
Egeria's journal makes constant references to events in the
Scriptures, particularly the Old Testament. She discusses
the Scripture with the bishop of Carrae, and tries to
interpret her reading of the Bible in light of his knowledge of the places in the area and the local lore he
offers. Her whole well-designed project of a pilgrimage to
the lands of the Bible makes no sense unless we assume that
she was Biblically well-versed, and knew what she wanted to
see. She is always commenting that "appropriate" psalms
and Scriptural passages are read when they reach a site,
and speaks of such an observance as her own wish(4). Her

ability to distinguish between what she has read and what is a non-Biblical tale also points to a woman of ecclesiastical culture and literacy, firmly established in a Christian culture, and eager to let her Biblical faith come alive.

One of the fascinating sidelights of Egeria's attitude to the Bible is that for her Old and New Testament are one continuous sacred taxt for the Christian. She calls various Old Testament figures "saint," refers to the bishop's instructions to the catechumens as enlightening them about the Law, and is interested in the sites of the Old Testament and New Testament places which are convenient to her travel route. Hers is not an attempt to retrace the steps of Jesus. She frequently asserts that her travels are in the name of God, and invokes the help of Jesus our God, she is rooted and grounded in the Bible of the Hebrews, which is hers and the foundation of her faith. Egeria does not, however, demonstrate any awareness of contemporary Judaism; her concern is for the Jewish tradition on a continuum with the Christian faith.

An important dimension of Egeria's character is her participation in a group of women whom she calls venerable ladies, sisters, my light, and perhaps also "your affection."[6] They belong to a movement of devout persons rather than an organized group of monastics.[7] They seem to have been virgins with some responsibility for the service of the church, Biblically and liturgically versed, bound by strong ties of affection and common interest, but also very unstructured in their freedom to move about and decide on the forms their devotion in the church would take. If one were to fix a role for them, it would be as spiritual forebears of the canonesses of medieval Europe, charged with proper observance of the liturgy in cathedral and other major churches. Egeria's writings testify to her certainty that they will be anxious to hear what she has to say about her journey, her discoveries about the Bible, and the liturgy of Jerusalem; she unquestioningly assumes that they will be still gathered together upon her return. Her relation to them is one of affection and care, as one can see not only from her terms of address, but from her exclamations ("But what more can I say ... you will never believe it, but ... just like at home.") Her tone and literary style is casual, addressed to friends who are awaiting something which will remind them of a friend, not only

impart information. Such a community must have been a very
supportive one, for they missed her (or least so she
expected), and were treated to such observations as Egeria's
exclamation that while she traveled from Jerusalem to
Constantinople, she was sure that they would understand her
making a mere twenty-five day side trip into Mesopotamia on
the way!

One can be reasonably sure that the Biblical and
liturgical concerns of her community were important in
Egeria's decision to come on her pilgrimage. She herself
speaks on several occasions about some of the reasons why
she is making her pilgrimage. She freqently says that she
has arrived in the "name of God" or "through Jesus our God."
(e.g., 23), and one must conclude that she believed that her
visit to the Biblical lands was in response to the call of
God. The very fact that she is writing back so faithfully
to her sisters about both the Bible and the liturgical
observances indicates, as has been suggested, that she also
felt that in some way she was going on behalf of her community.

She (like many others) goes to the holy places to pray
at Old Testament sites and martyrs' shrines there (e.g., 13).
Jerome articulated the sentiments of one going to pray in
the holy places in his letter about Paula, when he wrote of
the strengthening of devotion which such a journey can
provide for the devout. In a sense, she seems to have been
on a serarch for spiritual roots. Sometimes connected with
this motivation is the additional one of going to see the
holy monks, (17, 20) who as she notes several times, are
full of edifying teaching and discourse about the Bible,
and whose lives themselves are such eloquent testimony to
the faith. Another motivating factor must have been the
temperament of the author, for, as she once confesses
openly to her sisters, she is curious and likes to find out
the explanation of things (16).

Egeria also illuminates much about the status of
women at this period. The value of her contribution is
circumscribed by our awareness that Egeria was connected
with the highest strata of society, and had significant
wealth at her disposal. Even so, she demonstrates some of
the freedom a woman of her class could have. She traveled
widely, limited only by her own desires and the political

situation. As we have also noted, she is clearly in charge, and is solicitously attended by bishops, clergy, monks, other religious people, and escorts of soldiers when she needs them, discussing religious matters freely with those suitable people whom she meets. One detects not a twinge of subordinate feeling in Egeria; she is self-confident and assured, moving straight-forwardly towards her aims in a fashion which indicates that she intends to achieve them.

Because this point is often neglected, it is essential to underscore that Egeria's life also demonstrates that the devout ecclesial women of this period did not all follow monastic/ascetic lifestyles. With Egeria one finds none of the great fasting and emphasis on poverty which Jerome cultivated in the women of the so-called "Roman circle,"[8] and one could surely not say of her, as Gregory of Nyssa of his sister Macrina, that "obscurity was her glory."[9] Rather than assume that she is an aberant religious, or a lay woman, one must recognize that in the fourth and fifth century there were communities of devout women of significant Biblical and liturgical learning, one of whom entered into this lengthy journey not only for herself but also for her community. She and the community to which she belonged back along the coast of France or Spain were ancestors of the communities of canonesses whose stories have not yet been properly written.[10] It is unfortunate that we do not have any other major documentation about such women at this period.

Within this perspective Egeria's account of her reunion with an old friend at the shrine of St. Thekla, about a mile and a half from Selucium, introduces a kindred spirit for Egeria and her community. Marthana, who is called by Egeria famous throughout the East, is a deaconess and head of the group of virgins who live around the shrine. Marthana is the only person whom Egeria mentions by name rather than function, and is evidently a person for whom Egeria has great affection. Egeria's comment to her sisters assures them of the particular devotion paid to St. Thekla, a woman famous still in the fourth and fifth century as a follower of the Apostle Paul and teacher in her own right. It equally assures them of someone who is carrying on the living tradition of an ecclesial woman with authority and responsibility, as are they. On a more personal level, one might wonder if Marthana is not also the only one mentioned in the journal whom Egeria considers both friend and colleague, and ecclesiastical equal.

Egeria as a person is one of the liveliest and most charming individuals of the early church to come down through her own writings. Her interests and her status as woman remove her from the theological and disciplinary polemics of the period, and her journal shows a person of unflagging interest and tenacity, appreciative of the efforts made to help her in her quest, and possessing a clear mind which is able to understand and order those things which are of importance to her as a member of a community concerned with Scripture and the church's liturgy. Although she asks many questions, and points up what might be contradictions, she is not particularly critical in her outlook. This should not surprise us in an age which was prone to belief in the miraculous, when even such great minds as Augustine's unquestioningly recount tales of apparitions locating relics for the faithful to venerate.[11] Egeria is a reporter, not a critic, and her primary aim seems to have been the upbuilding of the faith of herself, her community, and most for the church served by that community in her land on the far edge of the ocean. After reading all the travel journals, guides, and accounts of this period, my own personal suspicion is that the Bordeaux pilgrim would be a bore, Jerome would be demanding and volatile, while Egeria would be a delightful companion, whose wholehearted and informed search for an understanding of the church in its present existence and Biblical roots would nurture the perfect spirit for such a journey.

Egeria's pilgrimage journal itself is divided into two major halves. The first part relates her travel experiences from Mt. Sinai to Constantinople and the second is a report of the Jerusalem liturgy when she was visiting there. Both of them are interspersed with her evaluations of and personal observations about the things and people she sees. That characteristic alone makes her journal unique in the literature of the period. Jerome wrote his Onomasticon, which Egeria most probably read, and several decades before her the Journal of the Bordeaux Pilgrim was written, but neither of these or later works such as the work of Peter the Deacon and Bede's On the Holy Places are much more than lists of sites and significant data. Egeria's is much more:

it is her diary of her pilgrimage, full of precise description, evaluation, Biblical references, local lore, and introductions to significant ecclesiastical persons of the area. That her intention is to do more than to give a list of the sacred places is clear from the bipartite construction of her journal, for she spends almost as much time, in the part of her journal which we have, discussing the liturgical observances of the Jerusalem church as she does with her travels. The living church rooted in the lands of the Bible is the focus of Egeria's concern, and thus she writes of both its places of origin and its present worship.

The first half of Egeria's journal relates her journey from Mount Sinai (the beginning of the manuscript finds her approaching Sinai on foot) to Horeb through the valley where the children of Israel zigzaged their way through the desert, if, as she notes cautiously, she may believe what her guides tell her. After reaching Pharan she returns through the valley and goes through the desert to Clysma, traveling from Epauleum through Magdalum in dangerous territory where they were escorted by soldiers. From there she rides on to various sites of the land of Goshen in Egypt to Tanis, where she casually mentions a prior trip she made to the Thebaid. Then she retraces her steps back to Jerusalem, where she stays for "some time."

Her second trip is from Jerusalem to Mount Nebo, where she rides through the plains and mountains of Arabia to Nebo, with its extraordinary view of so many significant scriptural sites. Then she goes by the banks of the Jordon to Sedina, the city of Melchezedek, to Thesbe, to Carneas, and then back to Jerusalem.

Her third trip, undertaken after she had spent considerable time in Jerusalem (three years) and decided it was probably time to go home, takes her the longest distance. She wishes to go to Mesopotamia to see the holy monks and pray at the shrine of St. Thomas the Apostle at Edessa, and so decides to undertake the mere twenty-five day journey on her way home through Constantinople. She traveled to Antioch up into Mesopotamia, having crossed the wide and rushing Euphrates, finally arriving at Edessa. After an eventful three day stay she is off to Carrae (Haran), where now is the shrine of St. Helpidius, whom Palladius mentions as an important monastic saint. Having

also seen the well of Jacob and other Biblical sites, she
returns to Antioch and from there sets out to Tarsus on to
Selucia after a week's break for reprovisioning the expedi-
tion. About a mile and a half from the city she finds the
shrine of St. Thekla, where she meets her old friend
Marthana, then returns to Tarsus from whence she goes
through Cappedocia, Galatia, and Bythinia to Chalcedon.
Finally she comes to Constantinople, where she is writing
her journal to her community, begging their prayers, hoping
for reunion with them, and casually mentioning that she is
going to make another side trip up to Ephesus to pray at the
shrine of John the Apostle. (One wonders if she ever did
return home, or if she kept making side trips.)

The second half of Egeria's journal is an account of
the Jerusalem liturgy and observances, encompassing the
clergy, laity (whom Egeria calls lay people or on one
occasion seculars), and monastics of various sorts who
live in or come to pray in Jerusalem. She begins by de-
tailing the daily prayers and observances in the churches
where the bishop presides, then the Sunday offices. In the
telling, it is apparent that the bishop and his clergy
provide the focus for the liturgical observances, the
monastics have their own offices which have their own forms
but are also fitted into the "cathedral" offices. Offices
are said at first dawn, daybreak, noon, three, and four
(the lucernare); the monastic offices as well as those of
the bishop, clergy, and people. She spends a fair amount
of time developing the Lord's day observances in Jerusalem;
at this period there is a great deal of preaching on Sunday,
a fixed lectionary is used at least some of the time, and a
great deal of time is spent at the various offices.

Egeria then outlines the observances of various
festivals in the Jerusalem, insisting on the appropriate-
ness of all the psalms, hymns, prayers, and Scripture
readings at all the offices in the fixed liturgical
calendar. She writes in detail about the festivals of
Epiphany, its octave, and the fortieth day after Epiphany,
a celebration of the dedication of the Lord in the Temple.
The paschal observance is very elaborately described. Lent,
each of the days of the "Great Week" before the Pasch, the
great vigil, the Pasch and its octave, and the fortieth day
after Pasch are all reported on in great detail. Pentecost
and the time after Pentecost are also described.

Apparently Egeria was quite struck by the course of instruction which the candidates for baptism in the Jerusalem diocese underwent, because she details both the form and content of the instruction. She also notes that preaching and instruction are made available to the polyglot diocese through translation, officially through a Syriac speaking deacon who translates the Greek speaking bishop's discourse for the Syriac, and unofficially through the many people who speak Latin and will interpret for those who understand only that language.

The last brief segment we have of Egeria's journal relates the festivities of the day of Dedication, when the Jerusalem diocese celebrates on the same day the finding of the true cross, the dedication of the Martyrium on Golgotha, and the Anastasis, as well as the dedication of Solomon's temple. The manuscript breaks off in the midst of a description of the celebration of the octave of this feast of Dedication.

Even a glimpse at this brief survey of Egeria's journal gives some idea of the great significance her work has for those interested in the liturgy and religious observances of early fifth century Palestine, the condition of the Biblical sites, and something about the architecture at this period.

Just a few words should be said about the translation. As I have mentioned there are presently in print two good English translations of Egeria's journey, which have much helpful supporting material and useful illustrations. Wilkenson's is a relatively free translation, which he thinks desirable for a document which was written in a style much like the spoken Latin of the writer, to be read aloud to a waiting community. Gingras', which is heavily annotated, is a much more literal rendition, and preserves much more of the Latin rhythm of Egeria's style. I have used the critical text of the Corpus Christianorum Latinorum series for my own efforts, and have tried to remain close to the language of the original, while trying to give a fairly conversational tone which seemed appropriate to a journal. In this way I have tried to strike a balance between the styles of Gingras and Wilkinson.

I have been particularly attentive to the patterns of Egeria's style, and have tried to reproduce them as closely as I could, assuming like most commentators of today that Egeria's Latin represents a style of writing which is ancestral to the vernacular literature which will begin to emerge a few centuries after her time. I have also attempted to reproduce as carefully as possible the liturgical and religious terms which Egeria used, rather than to translate them freely into more modern words, on the supposition that it is important to have Egeria's precise language before us. Notes in the text usually accompany any such important words. My only exception has been when a modern English term corresponds to Egeria's exact meaning, and nothing would appear to be gained by a literal translation.

NOTES

1. Discussions of the discovery of the text and substan-
tial introductions to major issues are found in the
critical Latin text found in the <u>Itineraria et Alia
Geographia</u>, E. Franceschini and R. Weber, ed. Corpus
Christianorum Latinorum, v. 175 (Vienna: 1965); Helene
Petre's translation and edition <u>Etheria, Journal de
Voyage</u>, Sources Chretiennes (Paris: Les Editions du
Cerf, 1948); John Wilkinson, <u>Egeria's Travels</u> (London:
SPCK, 1971); George Gingras, Egeria: <u>Diary of a
Pilgrimage</u>, Ancient Christian Writers (New York:
Newman Press, 1970). Helpful bibliographies are found
in all of these editions; Gingras contains a particu-
larly thorough and orderly one, 135-142. For some
information about Roman travel, see Mary Johnson,
<u>Roman Life</u> (Chicago: Scott, Foresmans and Co., 1957)
306-313.

2. Summaries of the debates about the issue of authorship
may be found in Gingras, 2-7, and Wilkinson, 3-8. The
question is highly complex and cannot be settled with
certainty, given the manuscript evidence presently
available.

3. Gingras, 12-15 and Wilkinson 237-239 provide a summary
of debate as well as their own theories. Archeological
information about the dates of construction of the
various chruches and shrines in Jerusalem would require
a date after about 390, giving particular weight to
Gingras' hypothesis. The mention of Marthana the
deaconess in Basil of Selucia's <u>Life of St. Thekla</u>
(II, 30; P.G. 85) among the list of eminent women who
have been connected with the shrine (implying that
she was dead) would indicate a date before the mid-
fifth century.

4. On page 138-9 Gingras lists some major studies about
pilgrimages of this period. The fathers of the
early church were themselves of differing opinions
about the value of the pilgrimage. For instance,
Jerome praises most highly Paula's forsaking of "house,
children, servants, and in a word, everything
connected with the world" (Letter 108), whereas

Gregory of Nyssa is suspicious of the need for and any possible benefits of trips to the Holy Land (Letter 2).

5. *Vie de Ste Macrine*, Pierre Maravel, ed. Sources Chretiennes (Paris: Les Editions du Cerf., 1971), 3.

6. Although the meaning of the word "affectio" is known in late Latin, it is uncertain to whom Egeria is referring in the journal. Is it a proper term designating a particular person or a collective noun referring to the whole community? I suggest the later, making it parallel with the term "my light." Egeria uses the phrase "your affection" quite frequently, sometimes independently from and other times associated with plural nouns certainly designating the community (e.g., 5, 10, 29).

7. Sr. Mary Lawrence McKenna S.C.M.M. in *Women of the Church* (New York: P. J. Kennedy, 1967) 17-20 offers some comments about the devout as distinguished from the clerics or the monastics. Use of these categories can prevent some very unhelpful comments about Egeria's status in the church. See Gingras, note 43, p. 171-2.

7a. Jerome, Letter 108.

8. Eg. Jerome, *Letters* 54, 107, 108.

9. *Vie de Ste Macrine*, 11.

10. For an introduction, see Joan Morris' *The Lady Was A Bishop* (New York: Macmillan Co., 1973) 9-15.

11. Frederich van der Meer in *Augustine the Bishop* (New York: Harper and Row, 1961) 527-557, discusses some of Augustine's reports of his beliefs in the miraculous, giving a perspective to some general assumptions of the time.

THE PILGRIMAGE OF EGERIA

1. ... Were pointed out according to the Scripture. In the meantime we were walking along and came to a certain place where the mountains through which we were traveling opened out into an endless valley, enormous, quite level, and very beautiful. Through the valley appeared the holy mountain of God, Sinai. The place where the mountain open out is next to that place in which are the "Tombs of Craving." [Num. 11:34] When one comes to this place, as those holy men who were leading us reminded us, "It is the custom, when people come here, for them to say a prayer when they first see the mountain of God." And so we did just that. From this place to the mountain of God it is perhaps four miles[1] all the way through the valley, which as I said is enormous.

2. The valley is indeed exceedingly large, extending up to the flank of the mountain of God. As far as we were able to estimate by looking, (and the told us) it is in length perhaps sixteen miles, and in width they said four miles. So we crossed the valley, in order to come near the mountain. This is the huge and very flat valley in which the children of Israel dwelt in those days when Saint Moses ascended into the mountain of God and was there forty days and forty nights. [Ex. 24:18] It is also the valley in which the calf was made, whose location is shown even today, for a great stone stands fixed in that place. [Ex. 32] This is that very valley, in the head of which is the place where, as he was grazing the flock of his father-in-law, God spoke twice to Saint Moses from the burning bush. [Ex. 3:1] This was our route: first we would ascend the mountain of God, which from here appears to offer an easier ascent, and then we would descend again to that head of the valley where the bush was because from there it is an easier descent from the mountain of God.

So it seemed satisfactory that having seen all which we wanted to, having come down the mountain of God, where we would find the burning bush, from there we would go on the route all through the middle of that valley which lay ahead of us with the men of God who would show us each single place in the valley which was mentioned in the Scripture. So we did. Then we left the place, where arriving from Pharan we said a prayer. This was the way that we traveled through the middle of the valley to the head and thus wound

85

around to approach the mountain of God. The mountain seems to be one all around; having gone in one sees that there are many, but the whole is called the mountain of God, and especially so is that one in the middle of them all which is the highest, where as it is written, the majesty of God descended. [Ex. 19:18, 20; 24:16] All those which were around are as high as any which I think that I have ever seen; but the one in the center where the majesty of God descended is so much higher than all of those that, when we had gone up it, immediately all those mountains which seemed so high to us were so far under us that they were like little hills. Certainly it is quite admirable, and I do think that it could not be without the grace of God that the middle mountain, specially called Sinai on which descended the majesty of God, though it is higher than all the other mountains, nonetheless cannot be seen unless you come to its very base, just as you are about to climb it. Having completed your desires and descended from it, then you see it facing you, something you cannot do before climbing it. But this I already knew before coming to the mountain of God because of the comments of the brothers, and after I had gone there, I clearly knew it to be so.

3.   Then on Sabbath[2] we went up the mountain, and coming to some monastic cells, where the monks living there received us very hospitably, providing us every courtesy. A church with a presbyter is there. There we remained for the night, and on the morning of the Lord's Day, with the priests and monks who lived there, one by one we began to climb the mountain.

These mountains are climbed with infinite labor, because you do not go up them very slowly in a circular path, as we say "in a spiral," but you go straight up the whole way as if climbing over a wall. Then one must directly descend each one of these mountains until you reach the very base of the central mountain which is called Sinai. So by the will of Christ our God, helped by the prayers of holy men who were going with us, and with great labor, it was done. I had to go up on foot because one cannot go straight up riding. Nonetheless one does not feel the labor, because I saw the desire which I had being completed through the will of God.

86

At the fourth hour we arrived at the top of the holy
mountain of God, Sinai, where the Law was given, in the
place where the majesty of God descended on that day when
the mountain of God smoked. [Ex. 19:18] Now in this place
the summit of the mountain is not very large. Nonetheless
the church itself is very graceful. When therefore by the
help of God we had ascended to the height and arrived at the
door of the church, there was the presbyter assigned to that
church coming to meet us from his monastic cell. He was a
healthy old man, and, as they say here, an "ascetic," and--
what more can I say--quite worthy to be in this place. Then
also other presbyters met us, and all the monks who live
around the mountain, that is, if they were not prevented by
age or weakness. In fact no one stays on the summit of the
central mountain, for there is nothing there except the
church and the cave where Saint Moses was. [Ex. 33:22] The
reading in this place was all from the book of Moses, the
Oblation was made in due order and here we communicated.
Now as we left the church the presbyters gave us eulogia[3]
from this place, fruits which grow on this mountain. Even
though the holy mountain Sinai is all rocky, not having even
a bush, still there is a bit of earth down by the foot of
these mountains, both around the central one and those which
surround it. There the holy monks through their diligence
put bushes and establish orchards or cultivated plots, and
next to them their dwellings, so that they may seem to
gather fruits from the soil of the mountain itself, but
nonetheless they have cultivated it with their own hands.

After we had communicated and the holy men had given
us the eulogia and we had come through the church door, then
I immediately asked them to show us each place. The the
holy men kindly agreed to show us all the sites. They
pointed out to us the cave where Saint Moses was when he
ascended into the mountain of God that he might receive
again the tables of the Law, after he had broken the first
one when the people had sinned. [Ex. 34; 32:19] Then they
showed us other places which we wanted to see, and also
ones which they knew better than we.

But I would like you to know, venerable ladies my
sisters, that from the place where we were standing, the
area around the church, the summit of the middle, it seemed
to us that those mountains which we had first ascended with
difficulty were like little hills. Nonetheless they seemed

87

boundless and I do not think that I have seen any higher,
except for the middle mountain which greatly exceeds them.
From that place we saw Egypt, Palestine, the Red Sea, and
the Parthenian Sea[4] which goes all the way to Alexandria,
and finally the infinite Saracen lands. It is scarcely
possible to believe it, but these holy men pointed out each
place to us.

4.   Having satisfied every desire for which we had
hastened to climb up, we began the descent from the summit
of mountain of God, in order that we might go up another
mountain which joins it, called "On Horeb"; there is a
church there. [IKings 19:9] Horeb is the place where Saint
Elias the Prophet was, who fled from the face of Ahab the
King, the place where God spoke to him, saying, "What are
you doing here, Elias?" as it is written in the book of
Kings. Even today they show there the cave where Saint
Elias hid, before the door of the church which is there; in
that place they also show the altar of stone which Saint
Elias set up to make an offering to God. The holy men were
gracious enough to show us each place. Then we made the
Oblation[5] and most earnest prayer, and the passage was read
from the Book of Kings. Indeed I have always wished that
when we come to a particular place, a passage from Scripture
is read about it.

Then when we had made there the Oblation, we went up
again to another place not far from there, pointed out by the
presbyters and monks. It is the place where Saint Aaron
with the seventy elders stood when Saint Moses accepted the
Law from the Lord for the children of Israel. In that place,
although it is not mentioned in scripture, there is a vast
circular rock, having a flat surface on top where the holy
men are said to have stood. In the middle there is also a
kind of altar made with stones. There we read the proper
passage from the book of Moses and sang a psalm appropriate
to the place; and thus having prayed we descended from
there.

Now it was getting about the eighth hour and we still
had three miles to go before we would pass through those
mountains which we had entered the evening before. As I
said above, we would not go out by the side through which
we had entered, because we were to walk to all the holy
places and monastic dwellings which were there, and thus

to come out at the head of the valley, which I spoke of
above, which lies below the mountain of God. Our way out
brought us to the head of the valley, because there were
many monastic cells of holy men and a church in that place
where the burning bush was; the bush is living even today
and is still sprouting. After descending the mountain we
arrived at the bush at about the tenth hour. This is the
bush I spoke of before, from which God spoke to Moses in the
fire, and in that place there are many monks' dwellings and
a church in the head of the valley. In front of the church
is a most agreeable garden, with an abundance of the best
water. In this garden the bush grows. They point out the
place adjoining it, where Saint Moses stood when God said
to him, "Loosen the strap of your sandal," and so forth.
By the time we had come into the place, it was about four
in the afternoon,6 and thus because it was already evening,
we could not make Oblation; but we prayed in the church and
also in the garden where the bush was; the reading was also
from the book of Moses according to our custom. Thus
because it was late we ate with the holy men in the garden
before the bush, and so we made there our resting place.
Early the next day we arose and asked the presbyters if they
would make the Oblation, and so they did.

        5.   Since that was our route, we went through that
middle valley which stretched before us. It is that valley
where, as I said above, the children of Israel camped while
Moses ascended the mountain of God and came down again. All
the way through the valley the holy men were showing us the
different sites. Indeed at the head of the valley, where
we had stayed and seen the bush from which God spoke to
Saint Moses in the fire, we saw also the place where Saint
Moses stood before the bush when God said to him, "Loosen
the strap of your sandal, for the place in which you stand
is holy ground." [Ex. 3:5] And so they were showing us
similar places of interest all along the way as we left the
burning bush. They pointed out the place in which was the
camp of the children of Israel in those days in which Moses
was in the mountains. They also showed us the place where
the calf was made; for a great stone is fixed even today in
that place. As we went along the way we saw facing us the
summit of the mountain, looking down upon the whole valley,
from which place Saint Moses saw the children of Israel
dancing in those days when they made the calf. [Ex. 32:19]

They also showed us a great rock where Saint Moses descended with Joshua the son of Nun, on which, being angry, he broke the tablets which he carried.

They pointed out to us how each one of them had dwellings through the whole valley, and the foundations of them are visible even today, fashioned into stone circles. They also showed us the place where Saint Moses ordered the children of Israel to run "from door to door" when he returned from the mountain. [Ex 32:27] They showed us the place where the calf which Aaron had made for them was burnt by Moses' orders, and the torrent from which Saint Moses gave the children of Israel drink, as it is written in Exodus. [Ex. 32:20] They also showed us the place where the seventy men received some of the spirit of Moses, and the place where the children of Israel coveted food. [Num. 11:25; 11:4] They showed us the place called "The Burning" because a part of the camp burned, and there the first stopped because of the prayers of Saint Moses. [Num. 11:3; Ex. 16:13-15] They also showed us where manna and quails rained on the people. [Num. 11:6, 31] Thus they showed us everything which happended in the valley which as I said, is below the mountain of God, holy Sinai, as was written in the holy books of Moses. It was too much to write everything down, because it could not all be retained. But when your affection reads the holy books of Moses, do carefully imaging all things which have been done there.

This is the valley where the Pasch was celebrated a year after the departure of the children of Israel from the land of Egypt, because in that valley the children of Israel sojourned a long time. [Num. 9:1-5] Here Saint Moses twice ascended and descended the mountain of God, and they stayed long enough that a tabernacle was made and everything shown on the mountain was done. [Ex. 40:17] We were shown the place where Moses first fixed the tabernacle, and in which everything was done which God had ordered Moses on the mountain to do. [Num. 11:34] At the far end of the valley we also saw the Tombs of Craving, in that place where we again returned to our route by the way we had come, through the mountains, as I told you above.

That day we also visited other very holy monks, who because of age or weakness were not able to go up the mountain of God to make the Oblation. Nonetheless, when we

had come, they most kindly received us into their dwellings.
Having seen all the holy places we wanted to, particularly
all the places the children of Israel touched going to and
returning from the mountain of God, and having seen all the
holy men who live there, in the name of God we returned to
Pharan. And although I ought always to give thanks to God
in all things, I will not speak about so many and great
things God deigned to confer upon me, so unworthy and undeserving, as to have traveled to all those places which
were not merited by me. But I also cannot thank enough all
those holy people who were so kind as freely to receive me
in their dwellings and even lead me to all the places that
I always sought from Scripture. Many of the holy men who
lived on or about the mountain, and were strong enough in
body, were kind enough to guide us all the way to Pharan.

6.   When we had come to Pharan, which is twenty-five
miles from the mountain of God, we had to stay there two
days before we could resume the journey. On the third day,
early in the morning, we went from there to a rest-station
in the desert of Pharan, where we had stayed coming down, as
I indicated before. Then the next day, taking water, going
a little further through the mountains, we came to a rest-
station which was just above the sea. There one leaves
traveling among the mountains and begins again to walk right
by the sea. Sometimes you are so close by the sea that the
waves hit the feet of the animals, and other times the
traveler is one, two hundred, or even more than five hundred
feet from the sea through the desert. In the interior there
is no road at all, but the sands of the desert are all
around. The Pharanites, who customarily walk there with
their camels, place guideposts for themselves from place to
place, and thus they walk by day by aiming at those signs.
At night, however, the camels watch for the guideposts.
And do you know what else? From habit the Pharanites walk
more carefully and securely in this place at night than
other people can travel in those places where there is open
road.

When we returned from the mountains to that place, we
came out into the place we had entered the mountains
originally, and we returned again to the sea. So too the
children of Israel, returning from Sinai the mountain of
God went back through the route we took, even to the place
where we came out from the mountains and reached the Red

Sea. From this point we went back again by the path we had taken. The children of Israel made there own way from this same place as it is written in the book of holy Moses. [Num. 10:12; 33:16ff] But we remained to Clysma by the same road and rest-stations. In Clysma we had to rest again, and to resume the journey from there, for our route through the desert had been very sandy.

7. I already knew about the land of Goshen from the first time I was in Egypt. Nonetheless I wished to see all the places where the children of Israel had been going out from Ramesses until they reached the Red Sea, to the place which now, from the camp which is there, is called Clysma. [Ex. 12:37ff] We wanted to go from Clysma to the land of Goshen, to the city in the land of Goshen called Arabia. It is so called from the territory, that is "the land of Arabia, the land of Goshen"; it is a part of the land of Egypt, but is much better than all of Egypt. [Gen. 46:34 (Septuagint)] It is four days through the desert from Clysma, that is, from the Red Sea, to the city of Arabia, and even though it is through the desert, each resting place has a fort, with soldiers and officers, who always led us from fort to fort.

During this journey the holy men who were with us, the clergy and monks, showed us every single thing which I was seeking from the Scriptures. Some things were on the left of us, others on the right of the route, others were a long way on the trip, yet others were quite near. I wish your affection to believe me, that as far as I would perceive it, the children of Israel went some distance to the right, then they returned to the left, then they went a bit ahead, then they came back again; and thus they made their way until at length they reached the Red Sea.

Epauleum was pointed out to us in the distance, and then we went to Magdalum. [Ex. 14:2 (Septuagint) Epauleum= Pi-Hahirot; Magdalum=Migdol] Now there is a fort there, with soldiers commanded by an officer, who govern there on behalf of Roman authority. As customary they escorted us to the next fort, and we were shown the location of Beelsephon-- indeed we went there. It is the plain above the Red Sea by the side of the mountain which I mentioned before, where the children of Israel cried out when they saw the Egyptians coming after them. [Ex. 14:10] They also pointed out Etham

to us, which adjoins the desert, as it says in the Scripture,
as well as Succoth. [Ex. 13:30; 12:37; 12:43] Succoth is a
small hill in the middle of the valley, next to which the
children of Israel pitched camp, for this is the place where
the law of the Pasch was accepted. [Ex. 1:11] The city of
Phithom, which the children of Israel built, was pointed out
to us along the same path; at this place we left the
Scaracen lands and entered the borders of Egypt. Now this
Phithom is a military camp.

Heroopolis, which existed at the time when Joseph
hastened to meet his father Jacob, as it is written in the
book of Genesis, is now a village, but sufficiently large
that we would call it a town. [Gen. 46:29] It has a church
and martyria[7] and many dwellings of holy monks. At each
place we had to dismount to see everthing according to our
usual custom. For this town, now called Hero, is sixteen
miles from the land of Goshen and is now withing the borders
of Egypt. The place is quite pleasant because a branch of
the Nile flows through it. So we left Hero, going on to the
city called Arabia, which is a city in the land of Goshen.
[Gen. 47:6] Of it Scripture says, "Gather your father and
brothers in the best land of Egypt, in the land of Goshen,
in the land of Arabia."

8.   Rameses is four miles from the city of Arabia. As
we traveled to the rest-station of Arabia, we passed through
the middle of Rameses, for the city of Rameses is now a
plain, with not one dwelling standing. Great was its cir-
cumference and it once had many buildings, for the ruins of
it, lying just as they collapsed, appear vast today. Now
there is nothing except for a great Theban rock, out of
which are two great carved stones, which are said to be of
Moses and Aaron, for they say that the children of Israel
set them up in their honor. There is also a sycamore tree
there which is said to have been planted by the patriarchs.
Now it is very old and therefore very small; nonetheless it
still bears fruit. Anyone who is ill comes there and takes
its twigs, and finds them helpful. We learned this from
the holy bishop of Arabia who referred to it. He also told
us the name of the tree, which is called in Greek dendros
alethiae, which we would translate "the tree of truth."
This holy bishop was kind enough to meet us at Rameses. He
is an older man, exceedingly religious from the beginning
of his monastic life, and affable, receiving pilgrims most

graciously. He is also very learned in the Scriptures.
Since he had taken the trouble to come out and meet us
there, he showed us everything there and told us about the
statues which I mentioned above, and also about the sycamore
tree. This holy bishop also told us that Pharaoh, when he
saw the children of Israel deserting him, before going after
them, entered Rameses with his whole army and burnt it all,
large as it was, and from there set off in pursuit of the
children of Israel.

9.   By chance we experienced a very pleasant event,
for the day we arrived at the rest-station of Arabia was
the most blessed feast of the Epiphany, and that same day
they would be keeping vigil in the church. And so we were
kept there two days by the holy bishop, a holy and true man
of God well known to me since the time I visited the
Thebaid. The holy bishop is from the monks, for from early
childhood he was raised in a monastic dwelling, and thus is
as learned in Scripture as he is without fault in his life,
as I wrote above. At this point we sent back the Roman
soldiers who had come with us through Roman authority,
escorting us all this time through unsafe places. Because
there was a public highway through Egypt, which goes through
the city of Arabia, running from the Thebaid to Pelusium,
we no longer needed to trouble the soldiers.

Thus we traveled there all through the land of Goshen,
wending our way through seemingly endless vineyards which
yield wine as well as balsam, and among orchards and
cultivated fields and many gardens along the banks of the
Nile, as well as many estates which were once the lands of
the children of Israel. What more can I say? I do not
think that I have ever seen a more beautiful territory than
the land of Goshen. And so from the city of Arabia we made
our way for two full days through the land of Goshen,
arriving at Tanis, where Saint Moses was born. [Num. 13:23]
This same city of Tanis at one time was Pharaoh's capital.
As I said above, I already knew these places when I
traveled from Alexandria to the Thebaid, but I wanted to
know better the places which the children of Israel
traversed going from Rameses to the holy mountain of God,
Sinai, and so I had to return again from the land of Goshen
and from ther to Tanis. Setting out from Tanis, we went
over a road I knew and arrived at Pelusium. Making our way
by each of the rest-stations of Egypt along the way we had

come, I reached the borders of Palestine. And from there, in the name of Christ our God, I again traveled some distance through Palestine and returned to Aelia, that is, Jerusalem.

10. After some time I wanted to travel again, and with the help of God I intended to go up to Mount Nebo in Arabia, to that place God ordered Moses to climb, telling him, "Ascend Mount Araboth, Mount Nebo which is in the land of Moab facing Jerico, and see the land of Canaan, which I am giving to the children of Israel as their possession, and you will die on the mountain you ascend." [Deut. 32:49-50] Thus our God Jesus, who does not desert those hoping in him, also deigned to effect my wish.

Setting out from Jerusalem we made our way with holy men, a presbyter and deacons from Jerusalem, and other brothers, monks, traveling all the way to the place on the Jordon where the children of Israel crossed, where Joshua the son of Nun led them, as it is written in the book of Joshua, son of Nun. [Josh. 3 & 4] They pointed out to us a slightly raised place where the children of Ruben and Gad and the half-tribe of Manasses built an altar, on that part of the riverside where Jerico is. [Josh. 22:10] Having crossed the river, we came to the city called Livias, which is in the plain where the children of Israel pitched camp in those days. Even today the foundations of the camp of the children of Israel, and the places where they dwelt, can be seen in that place.

Beneath the mountains of Arabia on the Jordan is a vast plain. This is the place of which it is written: "And the children of Israel wept for forty days for Moses in Araboth Moab, on the Jordan across from Jerico." [Deut. 34:8] This is also the place where after Moses passed away Joshua the son of Nun was filled with the Spirit of wisdom; for Moses had laid his hands upon him, as it is written. [Deut. 34:9] This is the place where Moses wrote the book of Deuteronomy. [Deut. 31:24] It is also the place where Moses, in the hearing of the whole assembly of Israel, spoke the words of the canticle in the book of Deuteronomy all the way to the end. [Deut. 32:1-43; 33:1-29] This is the place where Saint Moses, the man of God, blessed the children of Israel, each in order, before he died. When we reached the plain, having prayed, the appropriate part of Deuteronomy

95

was read to us, not only the canticle, but also the blessings which he said over the children of Israel. After the reading we said another prayer, and giving thanks to God, we left the place.

It was always our custom that when we had reached the place we wanted to go, first we said a prayer, then a selection from Scripture was read, then an appropriate psalm was sung, and we again said a prayer. We always maintained this custom, God willing, whenever we arrived at the place we desired to visit.

To complete the work we had begun, we hurried on to reach Mount Nebo. Along the way a presbyter of that place, Livias, guided us, because we had asked him to come with us from the rest-station because he know the area better. This presbyter told us, "If you wish to see the water which flowed from the rock, which Moses gave the children of Israel when they are thirsty, turn at about the sixth mile along the road." [Ex. 17:6; Num. 20:8] When he said this, we were quite eager to go, and immediately turned off the road according to the directions of the presbyter who was guiding us. In that place is a small church at the foot of a mountain which is not Nebo, but a nearer one which is not far from Nebo. Many monks who are truly holy are there; they are call aescetics.

11. These holy monks very hospitably received us, permitting us to come in and greet them. When we entered with them, they prayed with us, and kindly gave us eulogia, as they customarily give to those whom they hospitably receive. There, between the church and the monks' cells, from a rock flows a great stream of water, very beautiful and limpid, and of the most delicious taste. Then we asked those holy monks who stay there why this water was of such quality and taste. Then they said: "This is the water which Moses gave the children of Israel in the desert." We prayed here according to our custom, heard a reading from the book of Moses, and said one psalm. Then we set off towards the mountain along with the holy clerics and monks, who had accompanied us. Many of the holy monks, who dwell near that water and were able to undertake the task, kindly agreed to ascend Mount Nebo with us. Going forth from this place we drew near to the foot of Mount Nebo, which was very

high. The greater part could be climbed by riding a
donkey, but a small part was so steep that it had to be
climbed on foot. And so we did.

12.   We reached Mount Nebo, where there is now a small
church. Within that church, in the place where the pulpit
stands, I saw a slightly elevated place, about the size of
a tomb. Then I asked the holy men what it was. They
replied, "Here Saint Moses was placed by the angels, because
as Scripture tells us 'his tomb shall be known by no human
being'. [Deut. 34:6; Jude 9] Thus it is certain that he was
buried by angels. His tomb where he is buried, is shown
even today, for we were shown it by the older monks who
lived there, and thus we can show it to you." The older
monks told us that the tradition was handed down to them by
their predecessors in monastic life.

Soon we said a prayer and did everthing in each holy
place according to our customary order. As we were just
leaving the church, those who knew the holy place, that is,
the presbyters and holy monks, told us, "If you want to see
the places which are written about in the books of Moses, go
outside the doors of the church and from the summit where
there is a view, look attentively, and we will tell you
which are here and can be seen." We were pleased to hear
this and immediately went outside. From the door of the
church we saw the place where the Jordan enters the Dead
Sea, which appeared just below the place where we stood.
In the distance we saw not only Livias, which was on this
side of the Jordan, but also Jericho which is across the
Jordon. This is how high the place was where we stood,
before the church door! From there can be seen the greater
part of Palestine, which is the land of promise, and all
the land of Jordan as far as the eye can see. [Deut. 9:28;
Heb. 11:9]

On the left we saw all the land of the Sodomites, and
Segor besides; of the five cities Segor alone is standing
today. [Gen. 19:22 (Segor=Zoar)] There is a memorial there;
but of the other cities nothing is visible but overturned
ruins because they were turned into ashes. We were also
shown the place where the pillar of Lot's wife stood, which
was mentioned in Scripture. [Gen. 19:26] But believe me,
venerable ladies, the pillar is not now visible, although
the place is pointed out; but the pillar itself was said to

have been completely covered by the Red Sea. Certainly when we saw the place we did not see the pillar, and I would not wish to deceive you. The bishop of that place, that is, of Segor, told us it had been several years now since the pillar had been visible. The place where stood the pillar, which is now totally covered by water, is about six miles from Segor. Then we went out around to the right side of church, and there they showed us two cities facing us, Esebon, which was that of Sehon, king of the Amorites, and is now called Exebon, and the other that of Og, king of Bashan, which is now called Safdra. [Num. 21:26 (Esebon= Heshbon)] Then from that place they showed us from afar Fogor, the city of the king of Edom. [Num. 23:28; Josh. 13:20 (Fogor=Peor)] All those cities which we saw were located on mountains, but a little beneath the place looked flatter to us. Then we were told that in the days when Saint Moses and the children of Israel fought against those cities camps were pitched there, for signs appear there even now. Indeed, from the part of the mountain which I called left, which was above the Dead Sea, a very sharp mountain was pointed out to us, which formerly was called Watchtower of the Field. [Num. 23:14 (Septuagint) Josh. 13:20] This the mountain on which Balak son of Beor put the diviner Balaam to curse the children of Israel and God would not permit it, as Scripture says. And so after seeing everything we wanted to, we went back to Jerusalem, returning through Jericho and the same route we had gone.

13. After some time I decided to go on to the land of the Ausites in order to see the memorial of Saint Job, to pray there. [Job 1:1] I had seen many holy monks coming from there to Jerusalem to see the holy places in order to pray there, and as they talked about everything related to each of the sites they stirred up in me the desire of making the effort of visiitng those places, if indeed one can call it work when a person sees her wishes fulfilled. Thus I set out from Jerusalem with holy men, who kindly offered their companionship on my journey, as they also were going there to pray. Taking the road from Jerusalem all the way to Carneas is an eight day journey.[8] Now Job's city is called Carneas, but before was Dinhaba in the land of the Ausites, on the borders of Idumea and Arabia. [Job 42:17 (Septuagint)]

98

Going by this route I saw by the banks of the river
Jordan a beautiful and pleasant valley, with an abundance of
vines and trees because abundant and excellent water flows
there. In the valley is a large village called Sedima. In
the middle of the village, which is situated in the middle
of a plain, is a small hill shaped like a large tomb. There
on the top of it is a church, and below around the church
large ancient foundations remain; in the village many such
mounds are left. When I saw such a lovely place I asked what
this very pleasant place might be. Then I was told: "This
is the city of king Melchizedek, which before was called
Salem, but now, through a corruption of the word, is called
Sedina. On the hill which is in the middle of the village,
as you can see there is a church which is called in Greek
opu Melchezedek. [Gen. 14:18] For this is the place where
Melchezedek offered God a pure sacrifice of bread and wine,
as it is written in Scripture."

14. Upon hearing this, we immediately dismounted, and
right away the holy presbyter and the clergy of the place
graciously greeted us. As soon as they had received us they
led us to church. When we arrived there, according to our
custom a prayer was offered, then there was a reading from
the book of Moses, a psalm appropriate to the place was sung,
and another offered before we came down. When we got to the
bottom, we met the holy prebyter, who was old and well
instructed in the Scriptures, from his monastic days
assigned to the place. His life, we afterwards learned, is
praised by many presbyters and bishops and he is said by
many to be worthy to preside in the place where Saint
Melchezede, on coming of Saint Abraham, first offered God
pure sacrifices. When we came down from the church, the
holy presbyter told us: "You see those foundations which
you see around the hill. They are from the palace of king
Melchezedek. Even now if someong wants to build a house and
comes to these foundations, that person sometimes finds a
little silver and bronze. You see this road which goes
from the river Jordan to this village. This is the road on
which Saint Abraham returned as he was going back to Sodom
after having killed Quodollagomor, king of the nations;
there Saint Melchezedek met him." [Gen. 14:17-18
(Quodollagomor=Chedorlaomer)]

15. Then I remembered that it was written that Saint
John had baptized in Ennon near Salim I asked him how far

away the place was. [John 3:23] Then the holy presbyter
said: "Look! It is right here within two hundred
feet. If you wish, I can lead you there on foot. The
abundant clean water which you see in this village comes
from this source." Then I thanked him and asked him to take
us to the place, and so he did. We followed him on foot all
the way through a very pleasant valley, until we came to a
loverly fruit orchard, in the middle of which he showed us
a spring of the best and cleanest water which flows forth
vigorously. In front of this spring is a kind of lake where
it appears that Saint John the Baptiest ministered. Then
the holy presbyter said to us: "Today this garden is called
the Greek cepos tu Agui Ioanni, which you in Latin would call
the orchard of Saint John." Many brothers, holy monks from
many places, come that they may wash in this place. Once
more, as this spring, as in all the other places, we prayed
and read from Scripture, then sang an appropriate psalm. All
the things that we customarily did when we came to a holy
place; so we did there.

The same holy presbyter told us that even today, every
Pasch, all who are to be baptized in the village, in the
church which is called opu Melchiedek, are baptized in the
spring. They return early with clerics and monks bearing
candles, saying psalms and antiphons, leading all who have
been baptized from the spring to the church of Saint
Melchezedek. Then we, accepting eulogia from the presbyter
out of the orchard of Saint John the Baptist, and also from
the holy monks who had their dwellings in that fruit
orchard, and giving thanks to God, embarked upon our journey.

16. Going for some distance through the valley of the
Jordan, because for a considerable distance our route was
there, suddenly we saw the city of the holy prophet Elias,
Thesbe, from whence he received the name Elias the Thesbite.
[IKings 17:1] Even today in that place is the cave in which
the holy man lived, and there is the tomb of Saint Jeptha,
whose name we read in the book of judges. [Judges 12:7]
Having given thanks to God according to custom, we resumed
our journey. Going in our way, we saw a valley on our left
which appeared most beautiful. This valley was large, send-
ing a vast torrent of water into the Jordan. In this valley
we saw someone's cell, that of a brother, a monk. Then,
because I am curious, I asked what about this valley would
induce a holy man, now a monk, to build his dwelling here,

100

for I did not think that he would do so without a reason.
Then the holy men who had come along the road with us and
knew the place, said to us: "This is the valley Corra,
where Saint Elias the Thesbite found rest in the times of
Ahab the king. [IKings 17:3-6] When there was a famine, by
the command of God a crow carried food to him and he drank
water from this torrent. This torrent which you see running
from this valley into the Jordan is Corra." So giving God
thanks again for having deigned to show us everything we
desired, even though we are unworthy, we resumed our journey
as on other days. Making our way each day, suddenly on our
left hand we saw the lands of Phoenicia in the distance. A
large and very high mountain appeared, which extended a long
way . . . [a folio of the manuscript is missing here] . . .
. . . which holy monk, an aescetic man, having delt in the
desert so many years, found it necessary to descend to the
city of Carneas to inform the bishop and clergy of that time
of what was revealed to him, they found a cave into which
they had gone about a hundred yards, when suddenly as they
dug, a stone appeared. When they had uncovered the stone,
they found carved on the top "Job." Then a church was built
in that place for Job, as you see, so that the stone with
the body was not moved to another place, but it was so
arranged that the body might lie under the altar. The church
was built by some tribune whose name I do not know, and it
stands unfinished to this day. So we asked the bishop in
the morning to offer the Oblation, and he graciously agreed
to do so. The bishop having blessed us, we set out. Thus
we took communion, and always giving thanks to God, we
returned to Jerusalem, making our way through each rest-
station which we had traveled three years ago.

  17. Some time having passed, since I had already been
in Jerusalem for three full years and had seen all the holy
places in which I wished to offer prayers, in the name of
God I set my mind to returning to my native land. But I
also wished, God willing, to travel to Mosopotamia in Syria
to visit the holy monks who are said to be very numerous
there and are of such an estimable life that one can
scarcely believe the reports. I also wanted to pray at the
martyrium of Saint Thomas the Apostle, where his entire body
is buried, that is, Edessa, where he was sent by the Lord
Jesus Christ who had promised to do this after he had
ascended into heaven in a letter which he sent to King Abgar
through his messenger Ananias. This letter is preserved with

great reverence at Edessa, where the martyrium is, I wish
your affection to believe me that there is no Christian who
having traveled to the holy places which are in Jerusalem
does not also go to offer prayer here. This place is a
twenty-five day journey from Jerusalem. Because Antioch is
nearer Mesopotamia, it seemed opportune to me, God willing,
to go there when I returned to Constantinople through
Antioch, and from there I could go to Mesopotamia. And so,
God willing, it was done.

18. Thus in the name of Christ our God I set out from
Antioch to Mesopotamia, my route passing through several
rest-stations and cities of the province of Syria Coele,
whose capital is Antioch, reaching from there the borders of
the province of Augusta Euphratensis, and arrived at the city
of Hierapolis, which is the provincial capital of Augusta
Euphratensis. And because this is a bountiful city, very
beautiful and prosperous, I had to stop there because we were
not now far from the borders of Mesopotamia. Having traveled
fifteen miles from Hieropolis, in the name of God I came to
the river Euphrates, which Scripture very properly calls
"the great river Euphrates". [Gen. 15:18] It is vast and
somewhat terrifying, for its current runs as rapidly as the
Rhone river, except that the Euphrates is larger. Then
because we had to cross by boat, and large ones at that, I
stayed there about half a day more. From thence in the name
of God I crossed the river Euphrates, arriving at the border
of Mesopotamia of Syria.

19. And so again making my way through several rest-
stations, I came to the city whose name we find in Scripture,
Batanis, which is a city even today. The church, with a
holy bishop who is both a monk and confessor, has several
martyria. The city contains multitudes of people, for an
army with its tribune is based here.

Setting our from there, we arrived in the name of
Christ our God at Edessa. When we had arrived there, we
immediately went to the chruch and martyrium of Saint
Thomas. Thus having prayed according to our custom, and
having done all these things we habitually do in holy
places, we also read there some things about Saint Thomas.
The church there is large and very beautiful and newly
built, and truly worthy to be a house of God. Because there
were so many things there which I wanted to see, I had to

stay there three days. So I saw many martyria and also holy
monks, some living by the martyria and others having their
dwellings far from the city in secluded places.

Then the holy bishop of the city, a truly religious
monk and confessor, having hospitably received me, told me:
"Because I see, daughter, that you have taken such a great
work upon yourself, because of your piety coming even from
the ends of the earth to these places, we will show you
whatever you want, whatever it would please Christians to
see." First giving thanks to God, I then asked him to be so
kind as to do as he had offered. He first led me to the
palace of King Agbar, and showed me there a large portrait
of him, quite like him, they say, and as lustrous as if it
were made of pearls. Looking at Agbar face to face, he
seems to be truly a wise and honorable man. Then the holy
bishop said to me: "Here is King Agbar, who before he saw
the Lord believed in him as truly the Son of God." Next to
that portrait was one also made of marble, said to be his
son Magnus, whose countenance was also gracious.

Then we went into the inner parts of the palace, and
there were ponds full of fish, of sorts I had never seen,
of great size, luster, and good taste. The city has not
other water inside it than that which come forth from the
palace like a great silver river. So the holy bishop told
me about the water: "At some time, after King Agbar wrote
to the Lord and the Lord wrote back to Agbar through
Annanias, as it is written in this letter -- after some
time had elapsed the Persians came and camped about the city.
[Texts of the letter are found in Eusebeus, Ecclesiastical
History I, 13.] Immediately Agbar, with all his army, bore
the Lord's letter to the gate, and publicly prayed: 'Lord
Jesus, you promised us that no other enemy would enter the
city, and look, now the Persians are at war with us,' When
the king had said this, holding up this open letter in his
hands, suddenly there was a great darkness outside the city,
covering the eyes of the Persians who were now drawing so
close to the city that they were only three miles off.
Soon they were so thrown in disorder by the darkness that
they could barely pitch camp and surround the city from that
distance of three miles. So confused were the Persians that
they never saw through what part of the city they could get
in, but they did guard the city with soldiers completely
encircling it from three miles away, and they beseiged it

for three months. Then when they could see no way to get into the city, they decided to kill those who were inside the city.

Now that little hill which you see, daughter, above the city, at that time provided the city with water. Seeing this, the Persians diverted the water from the city and made it flow to this side where they had established their camp. On the very day, and even the very hour when the Persians diverted the water, these springs which you see in this place immediately by the command of God at once burst forth; from that day to this these springs remain here, thanks be to God. But the water which the Persians diverted at that very moment dried up, so that there was not even one day when they could drink it as they beseiged the city, as one can see even today. Never even to this day has one drop of water appeared there. And so through God's will, for he had promised that this would happen, they immediately left for their home in Persia. Ever afterward, when an enemy wished to come and do battle with this city, this letter was brought forth and read at the gates, and immediately, at God's pleasure, all the enemy are expelled."

Afterwards the holy bishop told me about where those springs burst forth, a place which formerly was a field in the city beneath the palace of Agbar. "The palace of Agbar was in a somewhat elevated place, as you can now see. Such was the custom at that time, that whenever palaces were built, they were constructed in elevated places. Then after these springs burst forth in this place, Agbar built this palace in the field for his son Magnus, the one whose portrait you see placed beside his father, in order that these springs might be included in the palace." After the holy bishop told me all this, he then said: "Now let us go the gate, through which the messenger Anannias came with that letter of which I spoke."

When we came to that gate, the bishop stood, prayed, and there read us those letters and again blessing us, said another prayer. That holy man also informed us that from the day the messenger Annanias came through the gate with the letter of the Lord, even to the present, they make sure that no one unclean or in mourning shall go through this gate, nor shall the body of any dead person be carried out through this gate. Then the holy bishop showed us the tomb of Agbar and his whole family; it was very beautiful, but old-fashioned. He led us to the upper palace, where at first King Agbar lived, and showed us the other places of interest. It was particularly gratifying to me to receive from the holy man both the letter of Agbar to the Lord and of the Lord to Agbar. And although I have copies of them back home, I was quite pleased to have received these here from him, least perhaps we have received less in our native land, for these are longer. So I accepted them. Thus if Jesus our God wills that I return home, you will read them, ladies dear to my heart.

20. Having passed three days there, I had to go all the way to Carrae, as they now call it. [Charra=Haran] But in Scripture it is called Charra where Saint Abraham lived, as it is written in Genesis that the Lord said to Abraham, "Go from your land and from the house of your father and go into Haran," and so forth. [Gen. 12:1] When I reached there, that is, Charra, I went immediately to the church which is within the city itself. I soon saw the bishop of the place, a truly holy man of God, himself a monk and confessor, who kindly offered to show us all the places we wished. Then he led us immediately to the church outside the city which is on the site where Saint Abraham's house was, a church made from its stones and on its foundations, as the holy bishop told us. When we had come into that church he prayed and read a passage from the book of Genesis, sang a psalm, and the bishop having said another prayer and blessed us, we went outside. He then kindly agreed to lead us to the well from which Saint Rebecca carried water. The holy bishop told us: "Here is the well from which Saint Rebecca gave water to the camels of the servant of Abraham, Eleazar." [Gen. 24:15-20] He consented to show us everything.

The church, which, as I said, ladies, venerable sisters, is outside the city, where once was the house of Abraham, now has there a martyrium to a certain holy monk called Helpidius. It was our good fortune to arrive there the day before the martyr's day of Saint Helpidius, nine days before the kalends of May [April 23]. On this day from everywhere within the borders of Mesopotamia all the monks come to Haran, even the great monks who dwell in solitude and are called aescetics, both for that feast which is very highly celebrated here, and for the memory of Saint Abraham, whose house was where the church now is in which is laid the body of the holy martyr. It was more than we had hoped to see these truly holy men of God, the Mesopotamian monks, whose reputation and life are heard of afar. I never thought that I would be able to see them, not because it would be impossible for God to grant this to me, because he has deigned to grant everything, but because I had heard that they did not come down from their dwellings except on the Pasch and on this day, and because these are the sort who do marvelous works. And I did not even know on what day was the martyr's feast, as I said. Thus, God willing, the day arrived for which I had not dared hope when we had come. We stayed there two days, for the martyr's feast and for seeing all the holy men who graciously agreed to receive me and speak with me, even though I did not deserve it. Immediately after the martyr's feast they are not to be seen there, because soon after nightfall they seek the desert and each of them goes to the cell where he lives. In this city, apart from a few clerics and holy monks, I found not a single Christian, for all are pagans. Just as we reverence the place where Saint Abraham first dwelt, honoring his memory, so also the pagans greatly reverence a place about a mile outside the city, where are tombs of Nahor and Bethuel. [Gen. 29:24]

Because the bishop of the city is very learned in Scripture, I asked him, "I beg you, my Lord, tell me something I would like to know about." He replied, "Ask what you will, daughter, and I will tell you if I know." "I know through Scripture that Saint Abraham with his father Terah and Sarah his wife and Lot his brother's son came into this place, but I have not read that either Nahor or Bathuel traveled here. [Gen. 11:31] I know that only the servant of Abraham afterwards came to Charra to seek Rebecca, daughter of Bathuel son of Nahor, for Isaac, the son of his master Abraham." "Truly, daughter, it is written as you have said in Genesis, that Saint Abraham came here with his family; the Canonical Scriptures do not say at what time Nahor with his family and Bathuel arrived here. [Gen. 11:31] But clearly at sometime afterward they must have come here, for their tombs are about a mile from the city. For Scripture testifies truly that the servant of Saint Abraham came here to receive Saint Rebecca, and again that Saint Jacob came here that he might take the daughters of Laban the Syrian." [Gen. 24; 28]

Then I asked him where the well was from which Saint
Jacob gave water to the sheep which were herded by Rachel
the daughter of Laban the Syrian. [Gen. 11:28]   The
bishop told me: "Within about six miles of here is a
place next to a village which then was the land of Laban the
Syrian; when you wish to go there we will go with you and
show it to you, for there are many holy monks and aescetics,
as well as a holy church in that place." I also asked the
holy bishop where was the place where first Terah and his
family lived among the Chaldeeans.   Then the holy bishop
responded: "The place of which you speak is from here ten
days journey into Persia.   From here Nisibis is five days,
and from there to Ur, the city of the Chaldeeans, is five
more days. But now there is now access for Romans there,
because the Persians hold the whole territory.   Particularly
this part which is on the Roman borders of Persia and
Chaldee is called Syria Orientalis." He kindly told me many
other things, as had also many other holy bishops and monks,
always about the Scriptures and the deeds of holy men, of
monks, that is; if they were dead, of the marvels they had
done, if they are still in the body, of what is done daily
by those called aescetics. [2Cor. 12:3] For I do not wish
your affection to think that the monks have any other stories
than those of the divine Scriptures and the deeds of the
great monks.

21.   After I had spent two days there, the bishop led
us to the well where Saint Jacob watered the herd of Saint
Rachel, the well being six miles from Carrae. In honor of
this well, a church has been built, very large and beautiful.
When we had come to that well, the bishop prayed, a passage
was read from Genesis, a psalm appropriate to the place was
sung, and having said another prayer the bishop blessed us.
We also saw there next to the well a very large stone lying
there which Saint Jacob moved from the well, which is pointed
out even today. [Gen. 29:10] No one else lives around the
well except clerics of the church which is there, and monks
who have their cells nearby. The holy bishop told us about
their lives, which were truly extraordinary. Then, having
prayed in the church, I went up with the holy bishop to the
holy monks in their dwellings, and I gave thanks to God and
to those who deigned to receive me when I had come there,
and to tell me things worthy to come from their mouths.
Then they kindly gave me <u>eulogia</u> and to everyone who was
with me, as is the custom of the monks to give to those
whom they freely receive in their cells.

107

Because this place is in a large field, the bishop could show me a very large village facing us, about five hundred feet from the well, through which our path went. This village, as the bishop informed me, was at one time the property of Laban the Syrian, and is called Fadana. The tomb of Laban the Syrian, the father-in-law of Jacob, was pointed out to me in this village, as well as the place where Rachel stole the idols of her father. [Gen. 31:19] And so, having seen everything, in the name of God, we said farewell to the holy bishop and monks who had kindly guided us to that place. We returned through the same route and rest-stations by which we had come to Antioch.

22. When I had gone back to Antioch, I stayed there for a week until everything necessary for the journey was prepared. So departing from Antioch and traveling through several rest-stations, I came to the province which is called Cilicia, whose capital city is Tarsus, the same Tarsus where I had been while traveling to Jerusalem. But because only three days from Tarsus into Isuria is the martyrium of Saint Thecla, I was quite pleased to go there, especially since it was now so near.

23. Departing from Tarsus, I came to a certain city on the sea-coast there in Cilicia, called Pompeiopolis. From there, passing through the borders of Isuria I stayed in the city called Corycus, and on the third day I came to the city which is called Selucia of Isauria. When I had arrived there, I called on the bishop, a truly holy man chosen from among the monks; I also saw in the same city a very beautiful church. Because it is about a mile and a half from the city to Saint Thecla's martyrium, on a flatish hill, I decided to go out there and stay overnight.

At the holy church one finds nothing except numberless monastic dwellings for men and women. I discovered there my very dear friend the holy deaconess Marthana, to whose life everyone in the East bears testimony, whom I had gotten to know in Jerusalem, where she had gone up to pray. She rules these monastic dwellings of aputactitae[9] or virgins. When she saw me, how can I tell you what joy it was to her or to me? But let us return to the topic.

Many monastic dwellings are on the hill, and in the middle there is a great wall which encloses the church in

which is very beautiful. The wall was erected there to
protect the church from the Isaurians, who are quite evil
and frequently steal, and would be likely to attempt something against the monastery which is established there.
When I had come there in the name of God, prayer was made at
the shrine and the reading was from the Acts of Thecla. I
gave thanks to God who deigned to fulfill all my desires,
though I am unworthy and undeserving.

I spent two days there, seeing the holy monks and
aputactitae, both men and women, who live there; having
prayed and made my communion. I returned to Tarsus to my
route, where I stayed for three days before I set out on my
way in the name of God. Traveling that day to the rest-
station which is called Mansucrene, which is at the foot of
Mount Tarsus. I stayed there. After climbing Mount Tarsus
the next day and making my way through several provinces I
had already traveled (Cappadocia, Galatia, and Bithinia) I
came to Chalcedon, where I stayed because of the very famous
martyrium of Saint Euphemia, which I have heard about for a
long time. The next day I crossed the sea and came to
Constantinople, giving thanks to Christ our God, who deigned
to grant this grace to me, unworthy and undeserving. He
granted not only my desire to go but also to travel around
to what I desired and to return again to Constantinople.

When I arrived there, I did not cease to give thanks
to our God Jesus, who had deigned to bestow on me his mercy
through each of the churches and the apostles and each
single martyrium, who which there are so many here. From
this place, ladies, my light, as I am writing this to your
affection, I have proposed to go up in the name of Christ
our God to Asia, to Ephesus, in order to pray at the
martyrium of the blessed apostle John. But if after this I
am in the body, if I have come to find out about other
places, either I will speak of them in the presence of your
affection, or certainly, if anything else occurs to me, I
will write you. You indeed, ladies, my light, deign to
remember me, whether I be in the body or out of the body.

24. Aware that your affection would like to know what
is done daily in the holy places, I certainly ought to tell
you. Each day before cock crow, all the doors of the
Anastasis[10] are opened and all the monozontes[11] and the
parthene,[12] as they are called here, and in addition also

lay people, man and woman, who wish to keep the morning vigil.
And from this time until dawn they sing responsively hymns
and psalms, as well as antiphons; and along with each hymn
say a prayer. Two or three presbyters, as well as deacons,
are responsible for coming each day with the monastics to
pray at each hymn and antiphon.

When it starts to become light, they then begin to say
the morning hymns. Then the bishop arrives with the clergy
and immediately they go into the cave and from within the
enclosed area he prays for everyone; he also commemorates by
name whomever he will; then he blesses the catechumens.
Afterward he prays and blesses the faithful. When the bishop
has left the enclosed area, all draw near to kiss his hand,
and as he is leaving he blesses them one by one, and so at
dawn all are dismissed.

Again at the sixth hour in a similar way everyone goes
to the Anastasis and sings hymns and antiphons while the
bishop is being summoned; he immediately comes and without
sitting down goes into the enclosure of the Anastasis within
the cave where he was in the early morning, and there he
first prays, then blesses the faithful as he is leaving the
enclosure, and again the people draw near to kiss his hand.
The same thing happens at the ninth hour as at the sixth.

At the tenth hour, which here is called <u>licinicon</u>, which
we call <u>Lucernare</u>,[13] the whole multitude again assembles at
the Anastasis; all light lamps and candles and it is very
light. The light is not brought in from outside, but is
taken into the interior of the cave, where within the
enclosure by night and day a lamp is always lit. <u>Lucernare</u>
psalms are recited for some time, as well as antiphons. Then
the biship is summoned, and he comes down and is seated, as
well as the presbyters with him, singing hymns and antiphons.
But when they are finished according to custom, the bishop
rises and stands before the enclosed area, that is, before
the cave, and one of the deacons makes a commemoration of
individuals, as is the custom. As the deacon says each of
the names, the many little children standing around always
respond: <u>kyrie eleison</u>, which we say: "Have mercy." Their
voices are many. When the deacon has finished everything he
has to say, first the bishop prays for everyone; and then
all pray, the faithful us well as the catechumens. Then
the deacon cries out that each catechumen, wherever standing,

110

must bow the head, and then the bishop, standing, blesses
the catechumens. Then he prays again and the deacon,
crying out, reminds each of the faithful standing to bow the
head. Then the bishop blesses the faithful and the dismissal
is given at the Anastasis. Each one comes to kiss the
bishop's hand.

Afterwards the bishop is led with hymns from the
Anastasis to the Cross, and everyone follows. When they
arrive there, first he prays and blesses the catechumens;
then he says another prayer, and blesses the faithful. Then
after this the bishop with the whole crowd goes behind the
Cross and there again they do what they had done before the
Cross. Each one draws near to kiss the bishop's hand, as
they had done in the Anastasis and before the Cross. Many
large glass lamps are hung everywhere, and many candelabra
are before the Anastasis, as well as in the front and behind
the Cross. There are multitudes of lights all around. This
is the daily rite for six days at the Cross and at the
Anastasis.

But on the seventh day, that is, the Lord's Day, before
cock crow the whole congregation gathers, all who can get in
the place, in the place just outside where lamps are hanging
for this purpose, as is done at Pasch, in the basilica,
which is next to the Anastasis. Because they are afraid
that they will not arrive before dawn, they come early and
sit there. They recite hymns as well as antiphons, and they
pray with each hymn and antiphon. Both presbyters and
deacons are always ready to hold the vigil in that place for
a congregation which has gathered. For it is the custom
that the holy places are not opened before dawn.

As soon as the first cock has crowed, the bishop
descends and goes into the cave of the Anastasis. All the
doors are opened and the congregation all goes into the
Anastasis where innumerable lamps are lit, and when in this
way the people have entered, one of the presbyters sings a
hymn and all respond; after this he prays. Another psalm
is sung by one of the deacons, who similarly prays, and a
third psalm is sung by one of the clerics, and a third
prayer is made with a commemoration of everyone. Then
having said psalms and prayers, censers are brought into the
cave of the Anastasis so that the whole basilica of the
Anastasis is filled with the odor. Then the bishop stands

within the enclosure, takes the Gospel book and goes to
the door. There the bishop himself reads the resurrection
of the Lord. As soon as he begins to read, everyone moans
and groans with so many tears that even the most hardened
person could be moved to tears because the Lord has endured
so much for us.

Having read the Gospel, the bishop leaves and is led
with hymns to the Cross, and all the people go with him.
There again he sings a psalm and prays. Then he blesses the
people and dismisses them, and as they leave they all go up
to the bishop and kiss his hand. Soon the bishop goes back
into his house, and from that hour all the monazontes return
to the Anastasis and sing psalms and antiphons until dawn,
and say a prayer after each psalm and antiphon. Each day in
turn presbyters and deacons keep vigil at the Anastasis with
the people. Of the laity, men and women, those who wish
stay in the place until dawn, and those who do not, return
to their homes to sleep.

25. When it is light, because it is the Lord's Day,
the congregation gathers in the great church which
Constantine built, the church on Golgotha behind the Cross,
and there they do what is everywhere the custom on the Lord's
Day. Indeed it is the custom here that all the presbyters
who have been seated and who wish may preach, and after all
of them the bishop preaches. Thus sermons are always given
on the Lord's Day, in order that the people may be educated
in Scripture and the love of God. Because of the preaching,
there is a long delay before the dismissal of the assembly,
and so the dismissal is sometimes not before ten or eleven
o'clock. But when the dismissal of the assembly is made
according to custom, as it is done everywhere, then the
monozontes led the bishop with hymns from the church to the
Anastasis. But when the bishop is arriving, accompanied by
hymns, all of the doors of the basilica are opened, and all
the people come in -- the faithful, that is, not the
catechumens. When the people have entered, the bishop comes
in and immediately enters the enclosure of the martyrium in
the cave. First they give thanks to God, and prayer for all
is made; afterwards the deacon calls out for all to bow
their heads, wherever they are standing, and so the bishop
standing inside the enclosure blesses them and afterwards
they leave. As they are going out everyone goes up to the
bishop and kisses his hand. So it is that the dismissal is
delayed until eleven or noon.

At _Lucernare_ all is done according to daily custom.
Thus the custom is observed carefully each day throughout
the whole year, except on solemn festivals, and we will note
later how they are observed. The most important of all their
rules is that appropriate psalms and antiphons are always
said, during the night as well as in the early morning. And
those during the day, at noon or three in the afternoon, or
at the _Lucernare,_ are always related to whatever is being
celebrated. During the whole year on each Sunday they
proceed to the major church on Golgotha behind the Cross,
the church built by Constantine; but on the Lord's Day which
is the fiftieth day,[14] everyone gathers at Sion, as you will
find described later. In order that they may arrive at Sion
before nine in the morning, first the dismissal is given in
the major church . . . . [one folio is missing here]
"Blessed is he who comes in the name of the Lord," et cetera.
Because of the _monozontes_ who come on foot, one must go
slowly, and so one arrives at Jerusalem at the hour when
people can just see each other, that is, when it is near
day-break but still before it. When all have arrived there,
the bishop immediately enters the Anastasis and everyone
with him, and the lamps are now all lit there. Then a psalm
is sung there, and a prayer, and then first the catechumens
and then the faithful are blessed by the bishop. The bishop
returns home and everyone else goes home to rest. The
monozontes stay there until dawn and sing hymns.

After the people have rested, at the beginning of the
second hour, everyone assembles in the major church which is
at Golgotha. The decoration on that day in the church of
the Anastasis, the Cross, and Bethlehem is beyond words.
You see there nothing but gold and gems and silk; if you
look at the curtains, they are also of gold-striped silk.
All of the church furnishing used that day is gold encrusted
with gems. How can I describe or estimate the numbers and
weight of candelabra, candles and lamps and other furnishing? What can I say about the decorating of building
itself, which Constantine, under his mother's supervision,
honored as much as his empire permitted with gold, mosaics,
and precious marble, not only at the major, but as well as
the Anastasis and the Cross and other holy places at
Jerusalem?

But let us return to the topic. The first service is
held in the major church of Golgotha. When they have

preached, and read all the lessons and sung all the hymns, everything being appropriate to the day, the dismissal from the church is given after this. All go to the Anastasis singing hymns, according to custom; and so the dismissal is given about noon. At the Lucernare that day things are also done according to daily custom.

The next day in a similar way all assemble in the church on Golgotha, and again on the third day. On the third day everyone celebrates with rejoicing until noon in the church which Constantine built. The fourth day is celebrated in Eleona, the church on the mount of Olives, which is quite beautiful and decorated in a similar way to the other churches. The fifth day is celebrated at the Lazarium, about a mile and a half from Jerusalem, the sixth day on Sion, the seventh day in the Anastasis, the eighth day at the Cross. During these eight days everything is celebrated in all these holy places with joy and ceremony, as I described above. In Bethlehem, however, through all the eight days each day is celebrated with joy and ceremony by presbyters and all the clerics of the place and the monozontes, who are assigned to the place. From the hour when everyone returns in the night with the bishop to Jerusalem, whatever monks are in the place keep watch, singing hymns and antiphons until dawn in the church in Bethlehem, because the bishop on these days must always hold the feast in Jerusalem. Because of the solemnity and joy of this day a great crowd gathers in Jerusalem, not only monozontes, but also lay people, men and women.

26. Truly the fortieth day after Epiphany is celebrated here with the highest honor. On this day there is a procession in to the Anastasis; everyone proceeds in and gives thanks in order with the greatest joy, as though on Pasch. All the presbyters and then the bishop preach, all from the Gospel passage where after forty days Joseph and Mary carry the Lord to the Temple and Simeon and Anna, the prophetess and daughter of Phanuel see him, and they speak about seeing the Lord, and of the sacrifice which the parents offered. [Luke 2:22-31] Afterwards, when all things have been celebrated in due order, according to custom, the sacraments are offered and the dismissal given.

27. When the Paschal season is coming, it is celebrated thus. Just as with us the forty days before Pasch

are observed, so here the eight weeks before Easter are
observed. This is why eight weeks are kept: because they
do not fast on the Lord's days and Sabbaths, except for the
one Sabbath which is the vigil of Pasch and on which one
must fast. Aside from the day there is no fasting on any
Sabbath during the entire year. And so when the eight
Lord's days and seven Sabbaths are subtracted from the eight
weeks (because it is necessary, as I said above, to fast one
Sabbath) there remain forty-one days on which to fast, which
they call here eortae, that is, Quadragesimas.[15]

Each day of every week, this is what they do: on the
Lord's Day at the first cock crow the bishop reads the
Gospel passage about the Resurrection with the Anastasis, as
is done every Lord's day, and they do the same at the
Anastasis at the Cross as they do every Lord's Day, and they
do as is the custom to do on the Lord's days, in the major
church called the Martyrium which is in Golgotha behind the
Cross. Similarly, the dismissal having been given from the
church they go the Anastasis with hymns, as is always done
on the Lord's days. When they have done all this, it is
eleven o'clock; the Lucernare is recited at its proper hour,
as always at the Anastasis and the Cross, as is done in
each holy place; there is no service at the ninth hour.

On Monday[16] all also go to the Anastasis at cock
crow, as during the whole year, and all is done in the
morning as usual. Again at the third hour they go to the
Anastasis and at the third hour they do what is performed at
the sixth, because during Lent they have an additional third
hour service. And so what is done at the sixth and ninth
hour, and at the Lucernare, as it is customary to do during
the whole year in the holy places. So on Tuesday all is
done as on Monday. On Wednesday they go during the night
to the Anastasis and do all which they usually do in the
morning, and also at nine and noon. At three in the afternoon - because it is always the custom during the whole
year to proceed on Wednesday and Friday at three o'clock to
Sion, because in this region unless it is a martyr's feast
they always fast on Wednesdays and Fridays, even the
Catechumens -- so at three o'clock they proceed to Sion.
Now if it should happen during Lent a martyr's feast occurs,
they still proceed to Sion on Wednesday and Friday at three
o'clock. But during the days of Lent, as I said above, on
Wednesday they gather at Sion where all is done according

to custom during the whole year as it is done at three
o'clock, except for the Oblation. So that the people may
always know the Law, the bishop and the presbyters preach
assiduously. But when the dismissal is given, all the
people lead the bishop from there to the Anastasis at the
hour of Lucernare. Thus they sing hymns and antiphons,
pray, and have the dismissal of the Lucernare from the
Anastasis to the Cross. The dismissal of the Lucernare in
those days, that is, during Lent, is always later than
during the rest of the year. On Thursday all is done in a
similar to Monday and Tuesday. But on Friday all is done
as on Wednesday, and so on the same way they go at three to
Sion, and similarly from there the bishop is led with hymns
to the Anastasis.

On Friday a vigil is celebrated in the Anastasis from
that hour when they have arrived from Sion with hymns until
the morning, that is, from the hour of Lucernare until the
next morning which is the Sabbath. In the early morning
the Oblation is offered in the Anastasis, so that the
dismissal may be before daybreak. All during the night they
alternately recite psalms with the responses or antiphons,
and different readings, which are extended into the morning.
The service,[17] that is the Oblation, which is done on the
sabbath at the Anastasis before sunrise, so that at that
hour when day breaks, the dismissal is being given at the
Anastasis. So each day of the week is celebrated during
Lent.

As I have said, the service is in the early morning on
the Sabbath, that is, before daybreak, so that they may
quickly be freed who are called hebdomadaries. The custom
of fasting during Lent is that those who are called
Hebdomadaries, that is, those who make "seven days", eat on
the Lord's day when the dismissal is given at eleven. So
having eaten on the Lord's day, they do not eat again until
the Sabbath morning, soon after they have communicated at
the Anastasis. For their sakes, in order that they may be
more quickly freed, the dismissal is given in the Anastasis
on the Sabbath before dawn. Although I said above that
because of them the service is in the early morning, not
only they communicate, but all in the Anastasis that day
who wish to do so may communicate.

28. The following is their custom about fasting here during Lent. Some, who have eaten something on the Lord's Day after the dismissal, that is, at eleven o'clock or noon, do not eat again for the whole week until the Sabbath after the dismissal at the Anastasis. Those are the ones who "keep the week." Having eaten on the morning of the Sabbath, they do not eat in the evening, but on the next day, the Lord's Day, they take breakfast after the dismissal from the church, at eleven o'clock or later, and do not eat again until the next Sabbath, as I have said above. Such is the custom here that all those who are, as they say here aputactitae, men and women, not only on the days of Lent, but during the whole, when they eat, eat only once a day. If there are some of the aputactitae who cannot fast the whole week, as I said above, they eat mid-week on Thursday. But one who cannot do this fasts two consecutive days during Lent: those who cannot do that eat each evening. No one demands that anyone do anything, but all do as they can. No one is praised who does more, nor is the one who does less blamed. For such is the custom here. This is the food here during Lent: there is no bread, for it is not permitted to them, nor do they taste oil, nor anything which is from trees, but only some water and gruel. As we said, things are done so during Lent.

29. At the completion of the week, a vigil is held in the Anastasis on Friday from the Lucernare, when everyone comes from Sion, singing Psalms, until the Sabbath morning, when the Oblation is made in the Anastasis. So it is done on the second, third, fourth, fifth, and sixth week as it is done on the first week of Lent. When there are the two weeks, including this one, left before Pasch, everything is done each day as on the previous weeks, but so that the vigil, which on the previous six weeks was in the Anastasis on Friday, during the seventh week on Friday is held in Sion according to the custom which was followed in the Anastasis during the prior six weeks. During each hour they sing psalms and antiphons appropriate for the place and day. But there, when dawn begins on the Sabbath, the bishop offers the Oblation in the morning. Now as the dismissal is given, the archdeacon raises his voice and says: "Let us all prepare today for one o'clock at the Lazarium." And so as one o'clock approaches, everyone comes to the Lazarium, which is at Bethany, is about two miles from the city. Going from Jerusalem toward the Lazarium, about a half a

mile from the place, a church is on the road at the place
where Mary the sister of Lazarus ran to the Lord. When the
bishop arrives here, all the monks hasten to him, and all
the people go in, and they sing a hymn and an antiphon and
read that place in the Gospel where the sister of Lazarus
met the Lord. [John 11:29] A prayer having been offered
and everyone having been blessed, then they go to the
Lazarium with hymns. When they have come to the Lazarium,
a great multitude gathers, not only there, but in the
surrounding fields, which are filled with people. Hymns and
antiphons appropriate to the day are recited here; in the
same way suitable Scripture passages are read. When the
dismissal is made, the Pasch is announced, that is, a
presbyter goes up to an elevated place, and reads the
passage which is in the Gospel: "When Jesus came into
Bethany six days before the Pasch," and so forth. [John 12:1]
This having been read, and the Pasch announced, the dismissal
is given. This is done on this day because it is written
in this Gospel that six days before the Pasch these events
occurred. From the Sabbath to Thursday, when after supper
the Lord was arrested in the night, is six days. Everyone
returns directly to the city and in the Anastasis the
Lucernare is celebrated according to custom.

30. The next day, the Lord's Day, begins the Paschal
week, which they call the Great Week. When the rites have
been celebrated from cock crow until morning, according to
custom in the Anastasis and the Cross, on the Lord's day the
people proceed according to custom to the great church which
is called the Martyrium because it is behind the Cross,
where the Lord suffered, and therefore is a martyr's shrine.
When all things are celebrated according to custom in the
great church, before the dismissal, the archdeacon calls out
and first says: "During the whole week which begins
tomorrow, let us come together to the Martyrium, the great
church." Then he speaks again and says: "Today at one let
us all be prepared to go to the Eleona." When the dismissal
is given in the great church, the Martyrium, the bishop is
led with hymns to the Anastasis, and there are done all the
things which it is the custom to do on the Lord's Day at the
Anastasis after the dismissal at the Martyrium. Then each
one goes home to eat a quick meal, so that by one o'clock
all will be ready to go to the church which is in Elona,
which is on Mount Olivet, where is the cave in which the
Lord taught.

31. At one o'clock all of the people go up to Mount
Olivet, that is, the Eleona, into the church: the bishop
is seated, they sing hymns and antiphons appropriate to the
day and place, as are the readings. And when it is about
three o'clock, they go down singing hymns to the Imbomon,
which is in the place from which the Lord ascended into
heaven, and everyone sits down there, for in the bishop's
presence all the people are ordered to sit down, so that
only the deacons remain standing. There hymns and antiphons
appropriate to the day and place are sung; similarly readings
and prayers are interspersed. When it is about one o'clock,
that place in the Gospel is read where infants with palms
and branches ran to the Lord, saying, "Blessed is he who
comes in the name of the Lord." [Mtt. 21:9] Immediately
the bishop rises with all of the people and then they all
walk from there to the summit of Mount Olivet. For all the
people walk before the bishop singing hymns and antiphons,
always responding: "Blessed is he who comes in the name of
the Lord." And whatever children in this place, even those
not able to walk, are carried on their parent's shoulders,
all holding branches, some of palm, some of olive; thus the
bishop is led in the same way that the Lord once was. And
from the height of the mountain all the way to the city, and
from there to the Anastasis through the whole city, all go
on foot, the matrons as well as the noble men thus lead the
bishop, singing responses, going slowly so that the people
may not tire. Then by evening they arrive at the Anastasis.
When they have arrived there, although it is evening, they
nonetheless say the Lucernare, and another prayer is said
at the Cross and the people are dismissed.

32. The next day, Monday, all which is customary from
cock crow until dawn, is done at the Anastasis, and at nine
o'clock and at noon as during the whole of Lent. But at
three o'clock everyone gathers in the Great Church, the
Martyrium, and there they sing hymns and antiphons until
seven in the evening; Scripture passages appropriate to the
day and place are read; prayers are interspersed. The
Lucernare is held there, when the time comes. Thus finally
by night they give the dismissal at the Martyrium. When
the dismissal is given they lead the bishop from there to
the Anastasis with hymns. But when he has entered into
the Anastasis, a hymn is sung, a praryer offered, the
catechumens blessed, then the faithful, and the dismissal
given.

33. On Tuesday all things are done as they were on Monday. One thing alone is added on Monday, that in the late evening, after the dismissal has been given at the Martyrium, and they have gone to the Anastasis and to the church which is on Mount Eleona. When they have arrived at that church, the bishop goes into the cave where the Lord was accustomed to teach the disciples, and he takes the codex of the Gospels, and the bishop stands and reads the words of the Lord which are written in the Gospel according to Matthew, where he says: "Watch that no one seduce you." [Mtt 24:4] Then the bishop reads the whole discourse. When he has finished he prays, blesses the catechumens, as well as the faithful, dismissal is given, and each one returns home for it is quite late at night.

34. On Wednesday everything is done during the whole day from the first cock crow on as on Monday and Tuesday, except that after the dismissal at night from the Martyrium the bishop is led with hymns to the Anastasis. The bishop immediately enters the cave which is in the Anastasis and stands within the railing; but a presbyter stands before the railing and takes the Gospel and reads the passage where Judas Iscariot went to the Jews that they might say exactly what they would give him if he would hand over the Lord. [Mtt. 26:3-16] While the passage is being read, there is great moaning and groaning among the people, so that there is no one who is not moved to tears at that hour. Afterwards a prayer is offered, the catechumens are blessed, and finally the faithful are dismissed.

35. On Thursday that which is customary is done from cock crow until the morning at the Anastasis, as well as at nine and twelve o'clock. At two o'clock according to custom all the people gather together at the Martyrium, but before the appointed time on other days, because the dismissal must be given more quickly. When all the people have gathered, everything which is appointed is done. The Oblation is offered at the Martyrium and the dismissal is mode at about four. But before the dismissal, the archdeacon calls out and says: "At the first hour of the night let us all gather at the church which is on the Eleona because great labor awaits us tonight." The dismissal having been given at the Martyrium the people go behind the Cross, and there a hymn is sung, prayer is made, and the bishop offers the Oblation and communicates everyone. Except on this one day out of

120

the whole year the Oblation is never offered behind the Cross. This dismissal having been given there, they go to the Anastasis, pray, and the catechumens are blessed they have come into Gethsemani, first a suitable prayer is offered, then a hymn is sung, and the place in the Gospel is read where the Lord was arrested. While this passage is being read, there is such moaning and groaning with weeping among the people that they can be heard by all the people of the city.

At that hour they go back to the city on foot, singing hymns; they come to the gate at the hour when people can begin to tell one person from another; from there all the way through the middle of the city each and everyone, old and young, rich, poor, all are ready, for particularly on this day no one leaves the vigil until day break. Thus the bishop is led from Gethsemani up to the gate and from there through the whole city up to the Cross. But when they have come there before the Cross, it is beginning to be clear daylight. Then they read the place in the Gospel where the Lord is led up to Pilate, and everything is written which Pilate spoke to the Lord or to the Jews. [John 18:28-19:16; Mtt. 27] Afterwards the bishop addresses the people, comforting them, because they have labored the whole night long and they are to work this whole day, encouraging them not to weaken, but to have hope in God, who will for this labor bestow on them an even greater reward. So comforting them as he is able, he addresses them: "Now go again, each one of you to your homes, sit there for a while, and be ready to be back here about eight o'clock, so that from that hour until about noon you may be able to see the holy wood of the Cross, which we believe to be profitable to the salvation of each of us. And from noon on we must again assemble here, that is, before the Cross, that we may devote ourselves to readings and prayers until the night."

37. After this, the dismissal is given from the Cross before sunrise, and everyone who is full of energy goes to Sion to pray at the column where the Lord was whipped. From there they go back to rest in their homes for a short while, and then are ready. Then the bishop's chair is set up on Golgotha behind the Cross, which now stands there; the bishop is seated on the chair, and before is placed a table covered with a linen cloth. The deacons stand in a circle around the table and covered with a linen cloth. The

deacons stand in a circle around the table and the silver
casket decorated with gold is brought in, in which is the
holy wood of the Cross. It is opened and taken out, and
both the wood of the Cross and the title are placed on the
table. While it is on the table, the bishop sits and
grasps the ends of the holy wood with his hnads, and the
deacons, who are standing around him, keep watch. Here is
why they guard it so. It is the custom that all of the
people here come one by one, the faithful and the catechumens,
bowing before the table, kissing the holy Cross and moving
on. I was told that because someone (I do not know who) bit
off and stole some of the holy Cross; now it is guarded by
the deacons so that it dare not be done by someone again.

So all of the people pass through one by one, bowing,
first with their foreheads and then with their eyes touching
the Cross and the title, and so kissing the Cross they pass
through, but no one is permitted to put a hand on the Cross.
But when they have kissed the Cross, they go on, and a
deacon stands holding a ring of Solomon and the horn from
which kings are annointed. They kiss the horn and venerate
the ring from about eight o'clock, and even until noon all
the people pass by, going in through one door and exiting
through another. This takes place where the day before,
Thursday, the Oblation was offered.

When noon comes, they go before the Cross, rain or
shine, because the place is outdoors and like a large and
very beautiful atrium, between the Cross and the Anastasis.
All the people are so crowded there that one cannot even
open a door. The bishop's chair is placed before the Cross,
and from noon to three nothing is done except that Biblical
passages are read. First there are readings from the Psalms,
whatever speaks of the Passion, then there are readings from
the Acts of the Apostles or from the Epistle, whatever speaks
of the Passion of the Lord, then places from the Gospels
where the Lord suffers, then readings from the prophets where
the speak of the Passion; then they read the Gospels where
he foretells the passion. And so from noon to three either
there are readings or hymns so that all the people may be
shown that whatever the prophets foretold of the Passion of
the Lord is done either in the Gospels or the Apostolic
writings. And thus during this three hours the people are
taught that nothing happened which was not first foretold,
and nothing was foretold which was not completed. Prayers

122

are always interspersed, and those prayers are always
fitting to the day. At each reading and prayer there is
such emotion and weeping by all the people that it is a
wonder; for there is no one, old or young, who does not on
this day weep for these three hours more than can be
imagined because the Lord has suffered for us. After this,
when it is about the ninth hour, the passage in the Gospel
of John is read, where he delivers up his spirit; after
that reading a prayer is offered and the dismissal. [John
19:30] When the dismissal is given before the Cross,
immediately everyone gathers in the great church of the
Martyrium and they do there those things they have been
doing weekly between three o'clock and evening, when they
gather at the Martyrium according to custom.

The dismissal having been given, they go from the
Martyrium to the Anastasis. And when they have come there,
the passage in the Gospel is read where Joseph asks Pilate
for the body of the Lord, that he might place it in a new
tomb. After the reading a prayer is offered, the catechumens
are blessed and the dismissal is given. On this day no
voice is raised to say that there will be a vigil at the
Anastasis because everyone knows that the people are tired,
but it is the custom that the vigil be there. And so, those
among the people who wish, or who can, keep vigil: those
who cannot, however, do not keep vigil until dawn. Those
of the clerics who are stronger or younger keep vigil until
dawn, and the whole night hymns and antiphons are sung there
until morning. A great crowd keep vigil, some from evening,
others from midnight, but all doing what they can.

38. On the Sabbath, the next day, all is done according
to custom at nine o'clock and again at noon; but three is
not observed as usually on the Sabbath; rather, the Paschal
vigil is prepared in the great church, the Martyrium. The
Paschal vigil is observed just as with us, but one thing is
done more elaborately: the infants,[18] when they have been
baptized and clothed, as soon as they come from the font
are first led with the bishop to the Anastasis. The bishop
goes within the enclosure of the Anastasis, sings a hymn,
and thus he returns with them to the great church, where
according to custom all the people are keeping watch.
Everything is done there which is customary with us, and
having offered the Oblation the dismissal is given. After
the dismissal of the vigil service they come with hymns to

the Anastasis and there again the passage of the resurrection gospel is read, and again the bishop makes the offering. But all is done quickly for the sake of the people, that they may not be delayed too long, and so the people are dismissed. On this day the hour of their dismissal is the same as with us.

39. These Paschal days are observed until late evening just as with us, and the services are performed in due order during the eight Paschal days as it is done everywhere during the Pasch. One finds the same decoration and arrangements through the eight Paschal days as at Epiphany, both in the major church and the Anastasis and the Cross as well as Eleona, and in Bethlehem and the Lazarium, for these are the Paschal days. All proceed on the Lord's Day first to the great church, the Martyrium, and on Monday and Tuesday; when after the dismissal from the Martyrium they all come with hymns to the Anastasis. But on Wednesday all proceed to the Eleona, Thursday to the Anastasis. But on Wednesday all proceed to the Eleona, Thursday to the Anastasis, Friday to Sion, on the Sabbath before the Cross, but on the Lord's Day, the octave, again to the great church, the Martyrium. Everyone of the eight days of the Pasch after lunch the bishop with all the clergy and all the new born, those who have just been baptized, and all of the aputactitae, male and female, and all the other people who wish to, go up to the Eleona. They sing hymns, and pray both in the church which is Eleona, where is the cave where Jesus taught the disciples, as well as in the Imbomon, which is that place where the Lord ascended into heaven. After they have sung psalms and prayed they go back down to the Anastasis for the Lucernare. This is done on all eight days. On the Lord's Day during the Pasch after the dismissal of the Lucernare from the Anastasis, the people conduct the bishops with hymns to Sion. When they have arrived there they sing hymns appropriate to the time and place, pray and read that place in the Gospel where the Lord, on the same day and in the same place where now the church of Sion is located, came into the midst of the disciples, even though the doors were shut. That was when Thomas, one of the disciples, was not present, and returning and being told by the disciples that they had seen the Lord, he said: "I will not believe, unless I see." [John 20:19-25] After this reading, a prayer is offered, the catechumens are blessed, then the faithful, and each one returns home late, about eight o'clock at night.

40. Then on the Lord's Day, the octave of the Pasch, immediately after noon all the people go up with the bishop to the Eleona; first everyone sits for a while in the church which is there, then they sing hymns and antiphons which are appropriate to the day and place, and pray suitably for the day and place. Then they go from there with hymns up to the Imbomon, and they observe things as at the Eleona. When the hour approaches all the people and the aputactitae lead the bishop with hymns to the Anastasis. They arrive at the Anastasis at the hour when the Lucernare is observed. The Lucernare is observed at the Anastasis as well as the Cross, and from there all of the people without exception lead the bishop with hymns to Sion. When they have arrived there, they as usual sing hymns appropriate to the time and place, then they read the place in the Gospel where on the Paschal octave The Lord entered into where the disciple were, and reproached Thomas because he had been unbelieving. [John 20:26-29] Then the whole reading is completed. When it is finished a prayer is offered; the catechumens are blessed, then the faithful according to custom, and each one returns home as on the Pasch, at about eight o'clock at night.

41. From the Pasch until the fortieth day, which is Pentecost, absolutely no one fasts here, not even those who are aputacttitae. For on those days all things are done according to custom at the Anastasis from cock crow to morning; likewise at the sixth hour and at the Lucernare. On the Lord's Day everyone proceeds as usual to the Martyrium, the great church, according to custom, and from three they go to the Anastasis with hymns. But on Wednesday and Fridays, because absolutely no one fasts here on these days, they proceed to Sion, but in the morning the service is performed according to the appointed order.

42. On the fortieth day after the Pasch, which is Thursday, the day before noon on Wednesday everyone goes to Bethlehem to celebrate the vigil. They keep the vigil in the church in Bethlehem, in the church where is the cave where the Lord was born. On the next day, Thursday, the fortieth day, the service is celebrated according to its usual order, so that presbyters and the bishop preach, saying words appropriate to the day and place. Afterwards in the evening everyone returns to Jerusalem.

43. The fiftieth day, which is the Lord's Day, provides
great work for the people. All things are done from the
first cock crow according to custom: vigil is kept in the
Anastasis that the bishop might read that place in the
Gospel which is always read on the Lord's Day, that is, the
resurrection of the Lord. Afterwards everything is done in
the Anastasis which is customary all year long.

When the morning has come, all the people proceed to the
great church, the Martyrium, where all things are performed
according to custom. The presbyters preach, afterwards the
bishop, and all prescribed things are done; the service is
completed as usual. But on this day the dismissal is given
sooner in the Martyrium, before nine o'clock. As soon as
the dismissal is given in the Martyrium, all the people,
down to the last one, lead the biship to Sion, in order to
arrive at Sion exactly at the third hour. When they have
arrived here, that place from the Acts of the Apostles is
read where the Spirit descends, that all the tongues which
were spoken might be understood. [Acts 2:1-12] Afterwards
the service is performed according to its proper order.
The presbyters read this particular passage because this is
the place on Sion (the church is something else) where after
the passion of the Lord a multitude gathered with the
apostles. Because the event mentioned above occurred, they
there read from the Acts of the Apostles.

Afterwards the service there is performed according to
its proper order, and is offered there, and then as the
people are dismissed the archdeacon cries out: "Today
immediately after noon let us all be ready in Eleona at the
Imbomon." All the people return home to rest, so that right
after lunch they may go up Mount Olivet, which is in
Eleona, each doing as much as possible, so that there is not
one Christian left in the city; all have gone. As soon as
they have climbed Mount Olivet, which is in the Eleona, first
they go into the Imbomon, which is in the place where the
Lord ascended into the heavens, and there the bishop, the
presbyters, as well as all the people sit. There they read
lections, sung hymns are interspersed, and antiphons
appropriate to the day and place are sung, for the prayers
which are interspersed are always so worded that they are
fitting to the time and place. The place from the Gospel
is read where it speaks of the Ascension of the Lord; there
is also a reading from the Acts of the Apostles which speaks

of the ascension of the Lord into the heavens after the
resurrection. [Mark 16:19; Luke 24:50-51; Act 1:4-13] When
this has been done, the catechumens are blessed, then the
faithful, and then at the other church on the Eleona, that
is in the cave in which the Lord had sat and taught the
Apostles. It is about four o'clock when they come there;
they have the Lucernare, prayer is said, the catechumens are
blessed and then the faithful.

Then all the people down to the last one go down from
there with the bishop, singing hymns and antiphons appropriate to the day; they very slowly arrive at the Martyrium.
When they have come to the gate of the city, it is already
night, and hundreds of church candles are brought out for
the people. Because it is quite far from the gate to the
great church, the Martyrium, it is thus about eight o'clock
when they arrive, because all the people walk very slowly so
that they will not be tired from walking. They open the
great doors which face the market place, and all the people
enter with the bishop into the Martyrium, singing hymns.
Having entered the church, hymns are sung, prayer is
offered, the catechumens are blessed and then the faithful;
and from there they go again with hymns to the Anastasis.

In the same way, when they have come into the Anastasis,
they sing hymns and antiphons, prayer is offered, the
catechumens are blessed then the faithful; a similar service
is held at the Cross. Then from there all the Christian
people down to the last one lead the bishop with hymns up
to Sion. When they have arrived there, appropriate
Scripture is read, psalms and antiphons are sung, prayer is
iffered, the catechumens are blessed and then the faithful,
and the dismissal is offered. When the dismissal is given
all go up to kiss the bishop's hand, and then all return
home about midnight. Thus the greatest labor is borne on
this day, because from the first cock crow vigil is kept at
the Anastasis and from there there is no ceasing the whole
day. Everything which is celebrated is drawn out, so that
only by midnight after the dismissal is made at Sion, does
everyone return home.

44. Now on the day after the fiftieth they fast
according to the custom, during the rest of the year, each
according to capacity, except on the Lord's Day, where in
this part of the world they never fast. On Ordinary days

127

everything is done as during the whole year, that is, as always the vigil is held from first cock-crow at the Anastasis. But if it is the Lord's Day, the bishop reads the Gospel according to custom in the Anastasis, the place of the resurrection of the Lord, where it is always read on the Lord's Day, and afterwards hymns and antiphons are sung until dawn in the Anastasis. If however it is not the Lord's Day, hymns and antiphons are sung until it is light in the Anastasis. The <u>aputactitae</u> all come, but from the people whoever is able comes. Each day however, the clergy by turns come from cock-crow; but the bishop always comes at daybreak that the service may be said at dawn, except on the Lord's Day when it is necessary for him to go at first cock-crow in order to read the Gospel at the Anastasis. Then at noon they do all which is customary in the Anastasis, as well as at three o'clock, and again at the <u>Lucernare</u> according to custom, as all year everything which is customary is don. On Wednesday and Friday at three o'clock according to custom there is always a service.

45. I should also write about the way those who are to be baptized at the Pasch are taught. Who ever gives his name, does so before the first day of Lent, and all the names are noted by the presbyters; this is before the start of those eight weeks which are, as I said, kept as the forty days. When all the names are noted by the presbyter, afterwards, on the next day of Lent, that which is the beginning of the eight weeks, the bishop's chair is placed in the middle of the great church, the Martyrium, and the priests sit on chairs and all the clergy stand about. One by one the "competent"[19] are led up; if they are men with their fathers, if women with their mothers.[20] The bishop questions individually the neighbors of each who has come up, asking, "Is the person of good life? respectful to parents? not a drunkard or liar?" He also asks about the more serious vices in a person. If the person is proved without reproach in all of the things about which the bishop has questioned the witnesses presents, he notes the person's name with his own hand. If however, someone is accused of anything, the bishop immediately orders the person to leave, saying "Change yourself, and if you do reform, come to the baptismal font." He makes such inquiries about both men and women. If however someone is a wanderer without witnesses who know the person, such a one will have a hard time being admitted to baptism.

46. However, ladies and sisters, I ought to write you so that you do not think that this is done without reason. It is the custom here that those who are preparing for baptism throughout those forty days are exorcised the first thing early in the morning by clerics as soon as the dismissal has been given the Anastasis in the morning. Immediately afterwards the bishop's chair is placed in the Martyrium, the great church, and all who are to be baptized sit in a circle around the bishop, men as well as women, while the fathers and the mothers stand there. All of the people who wish to hear may come in and sit down, if they are of the faithful. A catechumen, however, cannot enter when the bishop is teaching the Law.

The teaching is this way: Beginning with Genesis through those forty days he goes through the Scripture, first expounding carnally, then explaining spiritually.[21] The resurrection and all things about the faith are taught during those days; this is called catechesis. When five weeks of teaching have been completed, then they receive the Symbol.[22] He expounds the meaning of the whole Symbol as he did Scripture first carnally, and then spiritually. And so it is that in this place all of the faithful follow the Scriptures when they are read in church, because the catechesis is given during those hours. God know, ladies and sisters, that the faithful who have come in to hear the catechesis which is explained by the bishop raise their voices [in questioning] more than when the bishop sits and preaches [in church] about each of the things being explained. Dismissal from the catechesis is given at about nine and from there the bishop is led with hymns to the Anastasis and the service for nine o'clock in the morning is performed. Thus they are taught each day during the seven weeks.

But in the eighth week of Lent, which is called the Great Week, they are not called to be taught, because all things must be done which were described above. When the seven weeks have passed, there remains only the Paschal Week, which here is called the Great Week, then in the morning the bishop comes into the great church called the Martyrium. In the back, in the apse behind the altar, the bishop's chair is placed, and they come by one by one, each man with his father and each woman with her mother, and give back the Symbol to the bishop. After they have given back the

129

Symbol to the bishop, the bishop speaks to all and says:
"For all these seven weeks you have been taught all the
Law of Scripture and you have also hear the faith. You
have heard about the resurrection of the flesh, but of the
whole explanation of the Symbol, you could hear only that
allowed to catechumens. You are not yet able to know of a
higher mystery, that of Baptism because you are still
catechumens. Do not think that this is done without reason;
when you have been baptized in the name of the Lord, you
will hear about it through the eight Paschal days after the
dismissal in the Anastasis. But as long as you are
catechumens you cannot be told the more secret mysteries of
God."

47. When the Paschal days come, during those eight
days from the Pasch to the octave, as soon as the dismissal
is given from the church, they go with hymns to the Anastasis;
soon a prayer is said, the faithful are blessed and the
bishop stands, leaning against the interior railing which is
in the cave of the Anastasis, and explains everthing which
is done in Baptism. At that hour no catechumen may go up to
the Anastasis, only the neophytes and the faithful, who wish
to hear the mysteries, can go into the Anastasis. The doors
are closed, in order that no catechumen might come in that
way. While everything is being explained and discussed by
the bishop, the sound of the praises is so loud that it can
be heard outside the church. Such is his discourse that no
one who heard him would not be moved.

Because in this province a part of the people know both
Greek and Syriac, another part only Greek, and another only
Syriac, even though the bishop may know Syriac, he always
speaks Greek and never Syriac. Therefore a presbyter always
stands by him, who while the bishop is speaking in Greek,
interprets in Syriac that all may hear whatever is explained.
Because which ever Scripture passages are read in the
churches must always be read in Greek, someone is always
standing there who can interpret in Syriac, so that people
may always understand. Indeed, for those who are Latin,
knowing neither Syriac nor Greek, in order that they might
not be left in the dark, all is explained to them because
there are brothers and sisters who speak both Greek and
Latin who can explain it to them in Latin. But the most
pleasing and admirable thing here is that the hymns and

antiphons and readings as well as prayers which the bishop
says are so phrased as to always be appropriate and fitting
to the day which is celebrated and the place in which the
service is performed.

48.   The day on which the holy church which is on
Golgotha, called the Martyrium, was consecrated to God they
call the Feast of Dedications.   In addition the holy church,
which is at the Anastasis, the place where the Lord rose
after his passion was on that day consecrated to God.   The
dedication of these holy churches is celebrated with the
highest honor, because the cross of the Lord was found on
that day.   Because of this it was ordered that the holy
churches written of above would be consecrated on that same
day when the cross of the Lord was found, so that these days
may be celebrated with the greatest joy at the same time.
It was also found in Scriptures that the feast of Dedications was when Saint Solomon, in the completed house of God
which he had built, stood before the altar of God and prayed,
as it is written in the book of Paralipomenon. [Chron. 7:5-9]

49.   When this feast of Dedication comes, it is kept
for eight days.   For many days before a great crowd begins
to gather from all over, monks and aputactitae from various
provinces, such as Mesopotamia, Syria, Egypt, the Thebaid
where there are many monks, but also from all different
places and provinces, for there is no one who would not
come down this day to Jerusalem for such joy and such a
glorious festival.   Secular people, men as well as women
with a faithful spirit, also gather together in these days
in Jerusalem from the provinces for the holy day.   Although
fewer in number, there are forty or fifty bishops during
these days in Jerusalem, and with them come many of their
clergy.   What more can I say?   People think themselves to
have fallen into great sin if they are not at the solemnity
in these days, unless they have some urgent necessity which
would prevent someone from fulfilling a good intention.

In these days of Dedication, the ornaments of all the
churches are those used throughout Pasch and Epiphany, and
on each of the days they proceed to different holy places,
as on Pasch and Epiphany.   The first and second day they go
to the great church called the Martyrium.   The third day is
to the Eleona, where is the church on that mountain from

131

which the Lord ascended into heaven after the passion, and
within that church is that cave in which the Lord taught
the apostles on the Mount of Olives. On the fourth day . . .

NOTES

1. A Roman mile is about 5,000 feet. All references in this text to "miles" refer to the Roman measure.

2. Egeria habitually calls Saturday the Sabbath, and Sunday the Lord's Day, and I have retained that usage. Monday, Tuesday, etc. are called "second day," "third day," and so on. These days, because the terms have no liturgical significance, I translated by the ordinary English names to avoid unnecessary confusion.

3. Small blessed gifts, which were given as souvenirs to the pious pilgrims.

4. The eastern part of the Mediterranean ("the Sea of the Virgin").

5. Egeria seems to mean the Eucharistic service when ever she uses the term.

6. Romans measured 12 hours after sunrise; thus the length of the hour varied from season to season. In general, one should add or subtract six to the Roman hour, depending on the relationship to noon.

7. A martyrium is a shrine with relics of a saint, originally the shrine of a martyr.

8. Sometimes, as here, Egeria measures journeys according to the staging posts, which were a days ride apart.

9. Men and women monastics, from the Greek verb meaning "to renounce."

10. The Church of the Resurrection. I have used the Greek names which Egeria does, rather than translating into the vernacular.

11. Those who live alone.

12. The virgins.

13. The lamp lighting.

133

14. Egeria calls Pentecost "the Fiftieth Day."

15. Egeria's term for Lent.

16. Secunda feria, etc.

17. Most frequently by "missa" Egeria means the dismissal which marks the end of the service. Here on a few occasions "missa" refers to the whole service. The term does not yet have the technical sense of the Eucharistic service.

18. "Infants" refers to the newly baptized, regardless of chronological age.

19. The "competent" are those who are "seeking" baptism.

20. Here Egeria appears to be referring to sponsors or god parents who will guide these persons in their Christian life, not to the biological parents.

21. In this common terminology of the II-V century, by carnal is meant the literal sense, by spiritual allegorical senses.

22. The Symbol is, of course, the Creed of the Jerusalem Church.

INTRODUCTION TO EUDOKIA'S "MARTYRDOM OF ST. CYPRIAN"

The Life of Eudokia

Knowledge of the life of Eudokia is scanty although more plentiful than about any of the other writers in this book.[1] The earliest records indicate that she was the daughter of pagan philosopher Leontios who named her Athenais after the place of her birth, Athens. She seems to have been born about the beginning of the fifth century. All commentators agree that she was beautiful and learned; Leontios having carefully educated and steeped her in pagan culture.

For some reason Athenais went to Constantinople. It might be conjectured that the barbarian invasions which disrupted life in Athens during this time may have encouraged a moved to the wealthy and safe city of Constantinople, capital of the Eastern Empire, but no specific reason for the move has come to light. Somehow Athenais met Pulcheria, the older sister of the Byzantine Emperor Theododios II. There is a much later romantic tradition that Athenais came to Constantinople to plead for an equal distribution of her father's estate which her two older brothers were attempting to divide solely amongst themselves. There are several problems with this story. In the first case, support for the tale is not contemporary with the event but nearly a millenium later, and secondly it is doubtful that Leontios would have taken such care with the education of Eudokia if he had had two sons as well. In any event, through Pulcheria this young women was introduced to the equally young Byzantine ruler, and the two were married on June 7, 421. By this time Athenais had converted to Christianity, and the Patriarch Attikos had baptized her "Eudokia" which means "good will" or "good pleasure."

In 422 Eudokia gave birth to a daughter Licinia Eudoxia, and according to Socrates, a contemporary church historian, she wrote a poetic panegyric on the victory over the Persians by the Roman forces under the titular command of her husband. On January 2, 423 she received the additional name of Augusta from the Emperor as a sign of respect and honor.

The next reference to Eudokia comes in 431 when her second child, a daughter Flacilla, died. Around this time she seems to have made a vow to go on a pilgrimage to Jerusalem if she might witness the marriage of her daughter Eudoxia.

In 437 a political marriage was arranged for Eudoxia with the Western Roman Emperor Valentinian III, and it took place in Constantinople on October 29, 437. The following year Eudokia set out for Jerusalem to fulfill her vow. Along the way she distributed Largesse, and in Antioch she delivered a speech to the Senate and people which caused them to raise a statue of her. After a stay of some months in Jerusalem, she returned to Constantinople in 439 bringing with her the remains of St. Stephen.

Eudokia's activities in the next decade are particularly confusing, and various stories arose in Byzantine history to account for her departure from Constantinople while her husband was still alive. Some light can be shed on this problem if we know something about her husband.

Theodosios II had little interest in ruling, preferring to spend his time copying manuscripts. The successes of his reign, and there were several of lasting effect, were due primarily to the good counsel he received from his sister Pulcheria and his major administrative aids, the Prefects of the City. The various men who occupied this position were instrumental in constructing the land walls around the city, founding the University of Constantinople, and compiling the Theodosian law code.

A major governmental upheaval occurred in the years around 440, but what role Eudokia played in it is very hard to determine, since contemporary references are not forthcoming about the events themselves or their motivations. The story which grew up to account for the departure of the Emperess does not tie all the pieces together satisfactorily either historically or psychologically.

Supposedly Theodosios was presented with a huge apple on his way to church on Christmas Eve of 439 which he then gave to his wife. She in turn gave it to a certain Paulinus, Master of the Offices for her husband, a good friend of them both, either as a token of her love or as a sign of their affection for him. Paulinus, not knowing the apple had come originally from Theodosios, offered it to the Emperor as a sign of his own love and respect. The Emperor was furious and believed there was some illicit relationship between Paulinus and Eudokia, especially as she kept saying she had eaten the apple and not given it to Paulinus. Theodosios had Paulinus executed and banished Eudokia to Jerusalem.

This story is dubious for several reasons. In the first place Paulinus was not executed in Constantinople, but in Caesarea, over 350 miles from the capital. There is no explanation in the story for such a journey. Then, too, Eudokia's actions and motivations are not consistent with other accounts of her personality. She was known for her piety, and was therefore not likely to have had an affair with Paulinus nor to have offered the ridiculous lie that she had eaten the apple. And a story about an apple betraying a woman sounds like a modern retelling of the temptation in the garden. Furthermore we know that Kyros of Pannopolis, a poet and politician high in her favor, was consul the following year.[2] This would not have occurred if she were in disgrace. A more likely scenario is this: with the departure of Pulcheria from the court around the time of Eudokia's return from Jerusalem in 439, and by the execution of Paulinus in 440, the corrupt eunuch Chrysaphios came into prominence as Theodosios' major advisor. If Eudokia attempted to wield any power through her friend Kyros, this came to an end when Kyros was removed from the office of Praetorian Prefect of the East in the summer of 441. By the next year Kyros' supporters had ceased to be mentioned in court documents.

The departure of Eudokia seems to have occurred through a conjunction of several factors. Her influence at court, under the shadow of Pulcheria and the Prefects of the City, became negligible after the fall of Kyros. Then too her natural piety seems to have been arroused by her previous trip to Jerusalem and by her spiritual advisors, Severus and John. Finally the intellectual stimulation which she clearly enjoyed with Kyros and his circle ended.

Although her return to Jerusalem was permitted, there is fragmentary evidence that Theodosios was not happy in the separation. In 444 he is said to have sent his Count of Domestics, Saturninus, to Jerusalem to permanently

137

dispose of Eudokia's spiritual advisors which he did,
evidently believing them to be responsible for her with-
drawal from the capital. She, it is said, had this
Saturninus killed or killed him herself for his acts.
Official displeasure was not of long duration since she
continued to have money to spend on the construction of
churches and monasteries and other charities throughout the
remainder of her husband's reign (he died suddenly in July,
450). Her continued access to money also suggests that this
supposed murder never occurred.

While in Jerusalem Eudokia was not divorced from the
political and religious events of the last years of
Theodosios' reign, particularly from the Monophysite con-
troversy, a debate over the dominance of the divine nature
over the human in Christ. Chrysaphios and Dioscoros the
Alexandrian patriarch were very prominent in the pro-
Monophysite forces and they manipulated the Council of
Ephesus in 449 to condemn the writings of those church
leaders opposed to them, ignoring the letter of the Western
church leader, Leo. When Theodosios died, the Orthodox
Pulcheria came to the throne with Marcian, another Orthodox
Senator, and they forced a new council with the support of
Pope Leo, at Chalcedon in 451, at which the Monophysite
decrees of Ephesus were condemned and its leaders deposed.

Unfortunately for the government, the belief that the
divine nature was predominate in Christ had great appeal in
Egypt, Syria, and Palestine. Much civil unrest throughout
these areas followed the publication of the decrees of the
Council of Chalcedon. In Jerusalem, the orthodox patriarch
Juvenalis was deposed after first supporting the heresy
and then recanting, by a monk Theodosios who was supported
by Eudokia. Pope Leo himself in an extent letter (123)
dated June 15, 453 wrote to her asking for her support in
the cause of orthodoxy in the area. "I entreat the Lord
to gladden me with the news of your safety, and to bring
aid ever more and more by your means to the maintenance of
that article of the faith over which the minds of certain
monks within the province of Palestine have been much
disturbed.." From comments in another letter (117) Leo
also intended to get her son-in-law Valentinian III to
write to her as well. No letter to him has come down to us;
so, we do not know if a family approach was taken. In any

event, Eudokia held discussions with two noted holy men of
the region, Symeon the Stilite and Euthymios, and returned
to the orthodox faith in 455, taking communion from the
restored patriarch Juvenalis.

Throughout this period as well Eudokia continued her
patronage of churches, monasteries, and other charities. On
June 14, 460 she was at the consecration of the Church of
St. Stephen outside of Jerusalem, one of her major bene-
ficiaries. On October 20 of that same year she died and was
buried in that church.

Her Writings

According to the testimony of various late Classical
and medieval writers, Eudokia is supposed to have written
six works. These are poetic paraphrases of the first eight
books of the old testament (Octoteuch) and of the prophecies
of Daniel and Zachariah, a poem on the victory of her
husband over the Persians in 422, an address to the people
of Antioch, an Homeric Cento of the life of Christ, and the
"Martyrdom of St. Cyprian."

These six works form three classes of writings when
viewed from the perspective of firmness of ascription to
Eudokia. In the first class come the two paraphrases, the
"Martyrdom," and the speech in Antioch. In the second,
the poem on the victory over the Persians; and in the third,
the Homeric Cento.

The largest group of the works has continuously been
ascribed to her from late Antiquity. Indeed the mid-ninth
century Constantinoploitan Patriarch Photius mentions the
two Metaphrases and the "Martyrdom" in his Bibliotheca
(183, 184) even giving a resume of the plot of the latter
work which, since it is fragmentary now, is our only source
for the overall nature of the poem.

The victory poem is attested to in only one work, the
Ecclesiastical History of Socrates. If it weren't for the
earliness and the near contemporariness of Socrates' account,
more doubt would be placed on the likelihood of Eudokia's
authorship of such a work. None of her other known pieces
are on contemporary or military subjects. Since no fragment

139

of the poem is known, scholars weigh the probabilities of Socrates' account in her favor.

The Homeric Cento is ascribed to Eudokia by several late medieval Byzantine writers but by no writers contemporary to her. Although much of the Cento is extent, by its very nature, it is difficult to ascribe authorship to it. There is no doubt that Eudokia was capable of preparing such a work as the many Homeric references found in the "Martyrdom" suggest her great familiarity with the two epics of Homer. One mid-twelfth century historian John Zonaras wrote, however, that Eudokia merely completed the unfinished work of a Bishop Patricius, otherwise unknown, and it is this position which is generally accepted by scholars today and for that reason we are not including the piece in this anthology.

There is little to indicate when Eudokia wrote particular works except for the speech in Antioch and the victory poem. Arguments about pre-Jerusalem or post-Jerusalem hinge on the critics' opinion on whether the literary stimulus of Constantinople would have caused their writing or whether the religious atmosphere of the Holy Land would have encouraged the creation of pious works. "The Martyrdom" because of its interest with Antioch might well be from a time around 440, but we cannot tell for certain.

For the sake of completeness, and since the fragments are so short, here are the other known passages of Eudokia's writing: from the speech to the citizens of Antioch, "I claim to be of this race and blood," which is actually a direct quotation from Hippolochos' speech in Iliad 6 and Aeneas' speech in Iliad 20. From the Metaphrasis of the Octoteuch, "The Empress Eudokia, the daughter of the noble Leontios, worked on this second book of the righteous God."

"The Martyrdom of St. Cyprian"

The source for our text of the "Martyrdom" is one manuscript, the Laurentius VII, 10 in the edition of A. Ludwich from 1897. A 322 line first book and a 479 line second book have come down to us, but neither is complete, as the first begins in mid-sentence and the second ends in mid-sentence. From Photius, morever, we learn that there was a third book.[3]

As the "Martyrdom" has survived, book one is an examination of the temptations to which the holy virgin Justa was subjected by a certain magician, Cyprian, at the instigation of a lustful young man, Aglaides. Justa defeats the demons brought forward by Cyprian, and in the process so affects the corcerer that he repents of his evil ways and becomes a Christian. As the book ends he is the new Bishop of Antioch.

Book 2 is a monologue of Cyprian, recounting his life's story. He tells of his great training in the service of the pagan gods and goddesses and his work for Satan. He once again alludes to the attempted seduction of Justa, but this time the story is from his perspective. The tale breaks off just after he has rejected Satan.

From Photius' resume we learn that book one began with a presentation of Justa and her parents, how they were all converted to Christianity and how Aglaides came to fall in love with the virgin. Book two continued, we learn, with an account of the aid Eusebius gives to Cyprian during the doubting stage of his conversion, and concluded with a presentation of Cyprian's activities until be became a priest and was able to convert Aglaides.

Book three presented an elaborate picture of the martyrdoms of Justa and Cyprian under Diocletian and Maximius. After refusing to hide their faith, they were scouraged, then placed in a gigantic bronze frying pan and grilled over a fire. When they continued to sing happily during the grilling, a priest of the demons, by the name of Athanasius, was convinced that the fire was not hot, and he called on his gods to protect him as he walked through the fire. He was instantly reduced to ashes, however. Out of fear the local governor sent the two unharmed holy people to Nicomedia to the court of the Emperor who, in turn, condemned them to be beheaded beside the river Gallus with another holy man, Theoctistus. Friends of Theoctistus took the remains of the three martyrs back to Rome for burial in a temple built by the pious Roman matron Rufina, a relative of the Emperor Claudian.

German scholars from the late 19th and early 20th centuries have shown that Eudokia used a different prose work as a model for each book.[4] The three models are still

extent, the Conversio, Confessio and Martyrio Cypriani.
The Empress does not seem to have deviated much from her
sources, and many of the confusions of plot which we will
mention later can easily derive from the variety of her
sources which she did not carefully edit.

The "Martyrdom" as we have it is two separate scenes,
each independent of the other. One might consider them
as two panels of a triptych related, but not completely
overlapping, in subject. In book one the account of Justa
emphasizes the piety of the virgin in contrast to the evil
intentions of the demons. Much of the book is filled with
her prayers to the Lord for protection. Actions are held
to a minimum and then badly stated. Nearly twenty years in
the life of Cyprian is accounted for in the last twenty-five
lines of the book.

There is a decided change of emphasis from Justa to
Cyprian in book two, yet there is no transition between the
books. Book two suddenly opens with Cyprian talking at an
unknown place and time about himself. His life is a
progressive movement throughout the major pagan religious
and alchemical sites of antiquity: Athens-Mt. Olympus-
Ethiopia-Chaldea in which he gains greater and greater
knowledge of the workings of the universe. Two points need
careful consideration. The first is that most of the
physical forces which Cyprian learns about are controlled
by demons; and second, that Cyprian does not call the
knowledge he gains of them illusory or false. When he
decides to convert to Christianity, he sacrifices his con-
trolling knowledge of the universe as if it were of no
moment. Such lack of interest and doubt about the bene-
ficient operation of the universe were commonplaces in
classical antiquity and early Christianity. With determin-
ism prevalent in scientific thought at the time, astrology
was considered scientific. The Christian message rejected
determinism--without providing another scientific system to
replace it--and it rejected astrology. Eudokia and Cyprian
are in the mainstream of Christian thought on these issues
for their times: their attitude is difficult for more
modern readers to grasp.[5]

At the end of book one we notice that Bishop Cyprian
and Justa come to him so that he can honor her for her
contributions to his conversion to Christianity. These

honors are threefold: her name is changed to Justina, she is made a deaconess, and she is put in charge of a group of young women dedicated to the Lord. It was customary at this time as we noticed in reference to Marathana earlier, for deaconesses to be responsible for female communities rather than abbesses. Justina seems to have been one of these female leaders. It is difficult to refine more on Eudokia's meaning here as her wording in the passage is open to multiple interpretation: Eudokia writes that Justina is placed in the state of deaconship not that she is made a deacon or a deaconess. There is the added complication of an archaic ending whose meaning at the time of the writing is very hard to gage.

A final passage of some interest from the point of view of the early church is the scene of Cyprian's first visit to the church. We are given both lectionary readings and a partial order of worship: Psalm-Prophet-Psalm-Prophet-Epistle-Lord's Prayer-Homily-Dismissal of Catacheumans. Such an order is not unknown from this period, but outside literary support for it is not common.

Some comment must be made on the literary quality of the "Martyrdom of St. Cyprian." The Pauly-Wissova editor remarks that the poem is only of interest to the extent that it illustrates the decline which had occurred in the quality of Greek poetry in the later years of Antiquity.[6] It is difficult to disagree with this overall assessment of Eudokia's work.

Although Eudokia is not responsible for the original form of her models with their highly rhetorical speeches and descriptions, she did little to curtail their excessive length in her own work. Completeness and fullness were the goals of the rhetorical education which Eudokia received, not conciseness; thus the extensive apostrophes and petitions of Eudokia's prayers and the redundancy of Cyprian's experiences were not blemishes in the work from her perspective.

We mentioned earlier about inconsistencies of plot between the accounts of Justa's temptation in books one and two. The length of time involved is greatly different; the first presentation appears to occur in one long night whereas the second takes over seventy days. There are not visitations of specific demons in Cyprian's account while he does show much internal battling of the demons after Justa's victory. Cyprian's conversion is different as well. Book one presents it as immediate while book two suggests a more drawn out process. Some divergence might be accounted for as differences of point of view: what appeared as immediate to outsiders was the result of internal struggles for Cyprian. Other conflicts of fact such as the location of the events and the physical condition of Eudokia are harder to explain and suggest poor assimilation of the separate models.

Eudokia's work is not devoid of merit despite its roughness. Her knowledge and love of Homer are manifested throughout the poem in many Homeric word uses and references which serve to strengthen the fabric of the poem. She has used standard poetic devises, alliteration, assonance, chiasmus, felicitous word choices, metaphor and simile effectively in various sections of the "Martyrdom." A particularly fine simile occurs in Book two, lines 332-334 where Satan's acts are compared to "any weak and lame person doing battle seated on a horse who thinks well of his furious rushing and attributes great praise to himself." The metrics of the "Martyrdom" are a checkered matter. As the convention was at the time, long narrative poems were in sactylic hexameter -o o -o o -o o -o o -o o --. This rhythmic system was predicted on the difference between Greek vowels long and short by nature or position after two consonants or what are called double consonants. These rules had been codified centuries before the time of Eudokia, but unfortunately for poetry the spoken language continued to evolve after the rules had been formulated, and the nice distinction between vowels long and short by nature had become very indistinct. This would have had a serious effect on Greek poetry if the convention had not grown up to ignore the contemporary pronunciation and to treat the vowels as if they had retained traditional scansion. Eudokia was one of these authors who had to ignore modern pronunciation in meter. Sometimes she forgot, and there were syllables which were long or short strictly as convenience dictated. From time to time she indulged in altered spelling to keep the meter regular, and she employed archaic forms of words for the same end. Her most debilitating device which she used, however, was a frequent reliance on one syllable adverbs or conjunctions to fill out feet. Such words contributed little or nothing to the sense of the passage and prevented the development of strong rhythms which spanned several words. Subsequent to Eudokia's poetry, Greek poetry dropped dactylic hexameter as the meter for epic narrative and replaced it with iambic triometer. Several centuries later the entire edifice of long and short syllables was scrapped for the fiteen syllable accentual verse called "political" meter after its urban provenance. The "Martyrdom" is thus an example of a transition stage in Greek poetometrical development with both the problems and the rough hewn strength of such a state.

By bringing three separate traditions together in her poem, Eudokia has performed a unique service for those attempting to discover if Cyprian of Antioch really existed. In spite of all written evidence, and the stories exist in Greek, Latin, Syriac, Arabic and Coptic, no episcopal figures by the names of Anthemos or Cyprian held office in Antioch. Moreover, neither Cyprian, Eudokia, or Theoctistus figured in any martyriology until well into the Middle Ages (in the East, not before 886). Modern scholars generally consider the stories as pious fabrications for oratory and instructional purposes which grew up around the figure of the learned Cyprian, Bishop of Carthage (249-258), but eventually the tales took on a life of their own and were separated from the real Cyprian and ascribed to an imagined Cyprian of Antioch.[7]

In a broader cultural context Eudokia's literary activities were important in consolidating the influence of pagan learning on Christian writing. There had been great controversy on the merits of pagan literature and philosophy in a Christian age. Some Christian writers advocated rejection of such works as inappropriate influences on Christian writings, but Eudokia set a visible example to the contrary. It is not surprising then, that Sozuman in his Church History, written at the same time as Socrates' never mentions Eudokia and her writings for he was a supporter of the rejectionist school.

It is hardly possible to talk of modern influence of Eudokia's writings since they have not been readily available--this appears to be the first translation into English--, but what survived in Byzantine times was certainly read as we have noted. Other noble Byzantine women followed in her footsteps, moreover, including Cassia, the tenth century poetess, and Anna Comnena, the twelfth century historian. In her own time Eudokia was well-known in both East and West as Leo's letters about and to her indicate.

NOTES

1. A complete list of sources for the life and writings of Eudokia can be found in the bibliography at the end of this volume. The best resume of her life can be obtained from Pauly-Wissowa <u>Real Encyklopaedie</u> 6, 1, 906-912.

2. Extent poetry of Kyros of Pannopolis can be found in the <u>Greek Anthology</u>.

3. Photius, <u>Bibliotheca</u> 184.

4. Theodore Zahn, <u>Cyprian von Antioch und die deutsche Faustsage</u> (Erlangen, 1882) and F. Gregorovius, <u>Athenais, Geschichte einer byzantinischen Kaiserin</u> (1882).

5. Sambursky, <u>The Physical World of the Greeks</u>, trans. Merton Dagut (London: Routledge & Kegan Paul Ltd., 1963) is helpful for an understanding of the role of science and astronomy in Classical thought.

6. PW, 6, 1, 910.

7. T. A. Sabbatini, "S. Cipriano nella tradizione agiographica," in <u>Rivista de studi classici</u>, XXI (1973) is particularly fine in his study of this material.

THE MARTYRDOM OF ST. CYPRIAN

BOOK I

...With harsh words she sent away all the young men
because she had made Christ alone her successful suitor and
Lord.

Aglaides, having collected a mob in front of the
governor's palace, wanted to take the illustrious child by
force; but when they approached her, she cried out to Heaven.
Then the armed mob chased her out of her chambers, and she
immediately summoned a guardian spirit against Aglaides'
followers. Filled with passion and smitten by her charms,
and blind to the truth of the situation, Aglaides embraced
the young woman. She made the powerful sign of Christ, and
at once the shameless man was knocked flat on his back.
With her hands she tore at Aglaides' body, at his cheeks and
his curly hair. She rent his elegant clothes and laughed
scornfully at everything, following Thekla's example.
Afterward, she entered the house of the Lord.

The irate Aglaides besought the advice of an impious
magician, Cyprian by name, a man of evil deeds. Aglaides
promised him two talents of gold and glittering silver if
he could move by force the virgin who was unwilling to yield
to his friendliness. (Neither realized the power of the
untiring Christ.) The magician, pitying the miserable youth,
swiftly with an incantation called an evil demon.

He appeared in a twinkling, saying, "Why do you call
me? Speak."

Cyprian replied, "Fierce love for a Galilean girl has
tamed my heart. Tell me whether you are strong enough to
lead her into my bed for I greatly desire her." The foolish
demon nodded his assent, promising spectacular results with
the girl.

Cyprian then addressed his minion, "Tell me your
achievements so that I might have confidence in you."

He replied, "Formerly I was the bravest of the hosts
of angels, but I forsook the highest Lord of the seven
spheres of heaven.[1] You know what things I have done;

149

however, I shall speak of them. I stirred up through my evil divisiveness the foundations of the pure heaven, and I threw an array of heavenly inhabitants to earth. I even beguiled the mother of humanity, Eve, and I deprived Adam of the delightfulness of paradise. I myself forced the hand of Cain against his brother and covered the earth with blood. Thorns sprouted and the fruits of humanity were shameful because of me. I assembled sights hateful to God; I perpetrated frauds and deceptions. I inveigled mortal minds into worshipping ephemeral idols and into offering parts of shaggy bulls as sacrifices. I even stirred up the Hebrews to stretch fiercly on a cross the powerful Word of God, his Eternal Son. I have dashed cities together and shaken fiery walls; with delight I have wracked many beds with strife. Having accomplished all these things and countless others, how shall I not bring about the fall of this arrogant young girl?"

Consequently Cyprian rejoiced when the baneful demon said, "Take this herb and sprinkle it about the room of that respectable young woman, and I myself shall reach her and place a mind like our Father's [the Devil's] in her own breast. In her dreams she shall be persuaded to yield to you."

About nine in the evening the young woman was singing about the good God. Suddenly she shivered to her core for she recognized the demon's presumptuousness fanning a flame in her heart to divide her against herself. Swiftly, she thought of the Lord and prayed to him. Straightway she made the sign of the cross over everything in her room, and spoke eloquently, "Glorious God, Father of the spotless child Jesus Christ, and Master of all things, you who constrain the monstrous snake sent to hell in dusty chambers; you, most glorious one, who save all those whom he takes alive in his snares; you who stretching forth your hand to the starry heaven support the earth with its waters in the midst of the void; you who have granted fiery torches to the horses of Titan[2] and yoked the silvery moon to night; you who came to us in the form of a mortal man who opened for us the abundance of heaven; you who recoiled from the advice of that most dreadful beast, the snake of the forest-covered earth; you yourself sought our salvation, Lord, by your merciful spirit, healing completely our injury with your thorns, purifying all plans by the efficacious name of

Christ. Because of him the entire world appears rich, the
heavens expand and the earth is sustained, waters flow,
and all courses of life know you as the Lord Who Rules.
Come, save your servant by your power, least a terrible
reproach conquer me. I wish to remain, by your grace, a
holy virgin continuously, O immortal Worker. Heartily have
I loved you, Brightest Jesus, with great affection, my much-
praised Lord; for you kindle the flaming torch of your love
and dwell in my breast. You shall not tame your slave by
the hand of a horrible, loathsome, lawless villain, nor,
according to your promise, will you permit anything to
happen to me; but rather, ward off the sinful, invidious
words of that demon."

Having prayed thus, she armed herself with the sign of
God, and drove away the disgusting demon through Christ's
name: He sent the totally honorless demon flying.

The demon returned to Cyprian, the magician, with
great shame. Cyprian asked him, "Where is the maid whom I
begged you to bring me as quickly as possible?"

His agent replied, "I am confused. Don't ask about it.
I saw a fearful sign."

The magician smiled, and having been persuaded of the
difficulty of the task, called another malevolent demon,
Belial,[3] who spoke to Cyprian, "Tell me your evil command.
Your Father sent me as a helper in your distress."

At this the magician rejoiced, saying, "Demon, this is
your task: give this draught to the holy virgin. I shall
follow you, and I think she will be persuaded immediately."

The demon went.

The most holy virgin reverently addressed a prayer in
the middle of the night to the Lord, "In the middle of the
night I leap from my bed, O Glorious One, to speak aloud of
the sins I have committed in face of your righteousness,
justice, and truth. O bounteous giver of mercy and of
strong families, lawgiver to the atmosphere and protector of
the heavens whom the earth fears; you who have the power to
destroy his enemies, you the receiver of the sacrifice of
father Abraham as if it were a great hecatomb;[4] you who

151

threw down Baal and the murderous serpent and you who taught
all the Persian tribes to be holy through the service of
the holy Daniel; you who through your dear child Christ order
everything well and have kindled a light for the earth; you
who have led the dead after their destiny to light; I pray
to you, Lord. May you grant that we are not led into evils,
but rather protect me, Lord, that my body remain unharmed
always and that you permit me a life of virginity so that I
might see my wedding with our bridegroom Christ, and that I
might maintain my covenants which are of old: for yours is
the power and the glory and the honor. Amen."

After she had thus prayed, straightway the demon fled
with downcast eyes because of her courage. Coming ashamedly
before the magician, he stood there, and Cyprian asked,
"Demon, where is the virgin whom I begged you to lead to
me?"

He answered, "She overcame me with a strong sign which
when I looked at it, reduced me to a quivering, shuddering
mass."

Cyprian immediately called for another, more powerful,
higher ranking demon who was of the black-eyed race. He
said to him, "If you too are worthless, retire, powerless
one."

The demon boldly replied, "I shall lead that virgin to
you soon, so be ready yourself."

Cyprian responded back, "Give me a sign that you will
bring about a victory."

He replied, "First I shall drive her limbs to confusion
with fevers and after six days I shall stun her and on that
night I shall lead her to you."

The foolish demon went to the holy virgin, having first
made himself into the image of another virgin, similarly
clad. Then he sat on the bed, and spoke cunningly. "I
have come, like you, rejoicing in a lovely virginity, from
the place of Dawn, from which the Lord Christ sent me, that
He might perfect me thus. But beloved, tell me this, what
is the reward of your lovely virginity, and how much is the
cost? For indeed I see you are like a corpse, a dried up
body and a sapless trunk."

The meritorious young woman responded, "An immediate reward is worthless, for the better reward awaits me."

The godless demon said, "Was Eve a virgin in the garden of paradise with Adam? But when at last they united in bed, a mother of children, the first born of Adam, was revealed. From her came all of humankind, and Eve learned all noble things."

Then Justa, because she was paying attention to the demon, was on the brink of going out of the doors of heaven, and the accursed fellow rejoiced as he led the child of God astray.

When she recognized the trick of the baneful enemy, straightway she turned to prayer and immediately made the sign of the cross over her body. She cried out and drove the luckless, disgraceful presence from the house. After regaining some of her composure she said, "Grace from the Immortal One, I know; I have escaped a fiery illness." In prayer she said, "Christ, affix your gift of power to my body; may I stand in fear of you, Glorious One, and may you take pity on me in your righteousness, as I give thanks for your name."

Silently her sorrowful opponent faced the magician. Cyprian reproached him, "Did you too not fear the quick eye of the young women? But tell me, seeing the woman, what virtue is present in her?"

The vanquished demon replied, "Don't ask it of me nor inquire further. I am not able to explain the sign I saw; recoiling, useless because of my trembling, I fled precipitously away. But if you wish to learn something, she did swear a great oath."

Cyprian asked, "How might I swear this oath?"

The demon replied, "By the power to prevail which I have over everything."

As he heard this, Cyprian swore never to foresake this haughty one. Then the demon spoke boldly, "When I saw the sign of Christ stretched on a cross, I fled trembling."

Cyprian spoke, "Tell me, then, is he more powerful than you?"

Christ's opponent answered, "Hear me, and I shall speak truly: such things as we do through malice, leading human-kind into deceit, are available to all. But in this life the bent tool goes to the smith and is placed in the midst of the fire. So also if there were any sin, whether by angel or mortal, it is quickly announced to him, Christ hanging on a Cross."

Cyprian then spoke, "Begin, for I make friends quickly and take pleasure in speed. I yearn for the pleasures of the cross so that I shall not suffer further defeats."

The demon replied, "Having sworn a great oath, are you aware of your transgression in this request?"

He responded, "Speak, wretch, what oath have I just sworn to you?"

Spoke the demon, "An oath to my strong might."

The sorcerer answered, "Neither to you nor to your fearful works, evil one; this night I have perceived all truth because of the holy prayers of the young women and because of the worship of the powerful cross. For you are exceedingly feeble. Now I shall place a greater and power-ful sign on my body. I scoff at your friendship, and I renounce your commands." And as he said this he straightway offered homage to Christ and drove the malevolent demon away, saying, "Go far away, for I seek Christ." The evil left rapidly.

Cyprian put his books of magic on the sturdy shoulders of some youths to take to God's house, and followed them. There throwing himself at the feet of the holy Anthimos, he spoke as a suppliant, "Servant in the battle line of the Immortal heavenly Christ, I want to inscribe my heart in the book of life."

The enraged Anthimos answered, "From now on keep away from your evil ways for you cannot be relied upon. Keep out of the Lord's affairs for unconquerable is the power of the all-ruling Lord."

154

Cyprian responded, "I know that Christ's strength and power is greatest; for this very night I sent foul demons against a holy virgin to terrorize that dauntless young girl. But she who was knowledgeable conquered with prayer through Christ's sign. Now lift me up and have pity on me. Fearing for your suppliant, receive, O best of men, these books from which I wickedly brought about much evil, and burn them up in the fire. Take pity on my soul."

The priest, persuaded, took the books and burned them all, and then he spoke gentle words of good cheer to Cyprian, persuading him to approach God's sacred enclosure.

Then Cyprian went back to his own home, and burnt to ashes the forms of his feeble wooden images. He smote his body throughout the gloomy night, saying, "How dare I appear before Christ's eyes having done such evils? How might I praise God with my lips through which I have scoffed at others and summoned accursed demons?" Having scattered the ashes of his idols, he fearfully begged silently for the mercy of God to come to earth for him.

But when the silver and rosy footed Dawn of the great Sabbath comes, then rejoicing is everywhere. As a new convert of the great God, he went to the holy assembly and prayed as a learned man, "Ruler of all, if I am worthy to be your servant, I pray let me hear a word coming from your sanctuary, one of propitious omen from your written books."

When he reached the threshold of the temple, he heard the words of David, "O strong and glorious one, see, do not be silent, and receiving me, do not be far away." [Psalm 35:22] And the great prophet Hosea[5] uttered these inspired words, "If he leaves he will not be my servant." [Isaiah 52:13] David spoke again, "My eye looks to dawn, and light scatters the gloom of night so that I might always follow in your holy precepts." [Psalm 119:148] Isaiah said, "Fear of you does not wrack my breast, O my child Jacob whom I love and whom of all my other neighbors I choose first." [Isaiah 44:2] Paul inspired by God said, "Our Lord Christ himself redeems us from the earlier law of rough destruction." [Galatians 3:13] Again the excellent lyre player David said, "Who can utter the power of the immortal God and who can fill the ears of all with hymns to the Ruler of all?" [Psalm 106:2]

155

Then a prayer of the Lord with holy words, then the priest's homily followed; and then a human word was spoken, "Go out from the temple, those of you not fully instructed."

Cyprian humbly took a seat in silence. The deacon Asterios addressed him, "Leave the Lord's house."

He responded, "I am a servant of the crucified Christ, and you drive me away from here?"

The deacon said to him, "But you are not yet a full slave of the great God."

He said, "God lives always who reveals the vilest demons and who saves virgins, and he has pity on my heart. It is not fitting for me to leave this sanctuary until I am fully Christ's."

Learning these things Asterios went quickly to the bishop, a man beloved of the angels. Anthimos summoned Cyprian and spoke many firm words to him, to discover what he had done. Having prayed previously for his conversion, the Bishop was excited about the works God had done in the universe. Then he baptized Cyprian with the holy rites.

For eight days Cyprian read the holy scriptures of Christ. After twenty five days, humbled more, he was accomplished in the duties of the service, and became guardian of the doors of the holy mysteries. After twenty five more days, he was worthy to be a deacon. He powerfully tamed the battle array of the shameless, reckless, and godless demons, and he led many into the flock of Christ who rejected evil and blind faith in idols. After a year had elapsed, he obtained the chair of priest. Acting as a priest he waited sixteen years for the death of his elder.

The blessed, good bishop Anthimos summoned all his clergy. He spoke about how the assembly of Christ is the destinly of all, and the, still with a vision of heaven, he gave his seat to Cyprian. Then Anthimos, laying down his duties, went to the illustrious heavenly light.

Cyprian, now in charge of the glorious sanctuary of God, welcomed the virgin, honoring her with a deaconship and changing her name from Justa to Justina the blameless; and

he made her mother of all tender girls who were handmaids
of the Great God. Having protected many from disobedience
or unseemly worship, and persuaded them to yearn for Christ,
he awaited the trials for the glory of the most honored
Ruler of all. Amen.

NOTES

1. Seven Spheres of Heaven: in the cosmological scheme of antiquity each of the known planets, the moon, sun and stars had a separate sphere of movement around the earth.

2. Horses of Titan: either Apollo, the sun-god of later antiquity and offspring of a Titan, drives a chariot which pulls the sun across the heavens or Hyperion, a Titan who performed the same task according to earlier writers.

3. Belial is another name for Satan, derived from the passage in 2 Corinthians 6:15 and Intertestimental Hebrew literature.

4. Hecatomb: the sacrifice of 100 oxen to a god; a particularly great sacrifice.

5. Hosea: this reference is actually to Isaiah.

THE MARTYRDOM OF ST. CYPRIAN

BOOK II

Consider how many are interested in the solemn ritual
of faith in our treasured Christ; see my large tears so that
you learn from whence my pain comes; I know clearly that
you know. I am telling the truth. Notice how many delight
in shameful idols; I shall speak out about their wiliness.
For no other person among our people so followed superstition, accompanied demons, was an attendant of false idols,
nor did anyone else so well learn about them or their power.

I was that Cyprian whose parents had once dedicated him
to Apollo.[1] While a youngster I learned the secret rites of
the Nedyporain monster.[2] Then at seven I was again offered
to the Mithraic Phoebus;[3] I dwelled in the towering city of
the well-born Athenians since the time my parents lived
there.

At the age of ten I bound fast a torch of Zeus[4] and
bore the white mourning of Kore.[5] I performed the snake
rites which occurred on the Citadel of Athens.[6] Having been
a temple attendant I went to the temple of Mt. Olympus[7]
which those ignorant ones say is the precinct of their
feeble deities. There I heard the dull echo of their words.
I saw the grass, stumps and such marvelous sights which the
terrible evil-doing demons look after. I saw the seasons
going by and the changing storms, and many effects which the
meddlesome and cruel evil spirits fabricate by delusion. I
beheld the great shameless dance of the singers and the
others who battled in the crowds. I saw some ambushed,
frightened, or jeered at. I saw clearly the battle array of
the gods and the saints for I tarried there forty-eight days.
Then spirits in the air were sent out from the powerful
kingdoms over the land and all nations to do the worst and
most unseemly deeds they wished. When the sun went down, I
ate the tips of shrubs from blooming trees.

When I reached fifteen I was a disciple of all the
spirits and gods, and I knew about the seven levels of
priests and the deeds of the lawless demons. For my parents
strove that I might learn whatever there was to know about
the earth, air and sea, not only how the corruption of men

increases, but also what makes a plant good, sturdy, and nourishing; and what presses on the feeble body of humans and what the malignant villain finds, that very wily serpent, ruler of this acreage, that I might slight in conflict the wish of the deathless ruler.

I was then in the large horse-grazing land of Argos,[8] where were the white-clad rites of the Tithonian Dawn.[9] I was an initiate, and on the spot I saw the girdle of mists and wind of the much convoluted heaven, the kinship between water, well-nourished farm land, and the watery stream of celestial ether.

I went then to Elis, and I saw in Sparta the mighty wooden image of the Caledonian bull huntress, Artemis,[10] that I might know the woods, multiform nature, gemstones, writing and characters, and the ancient lore of the universe.

Coming to the land of Phrygia[11] I was a very wise diviner, knowing what ought to be done with livers and hearts; from the Scythians[12] I learned of the echoing sounds of birds and the gyrations of their flights, of the omens of youths who were foreseen, of boomings from wood and rocks, and of voices emanating from the dead, of the thud of doors, the quiver of human parts and of bodies suffused with blood and with defiled limbs; just as the food of ants comes from joints; of the visible pains of the body; of the monuments of nature, what has been truthfully and falsely sworn, and what counsels might prevent rest. The activities of the land, air, and depths of the sea were not hidden from me, neither changing phantasms nor minds, plotting, wily and full of cares, nor mechanically inclined, either weakly fraudulent or doing any kind of evil you find on earth.

When my twentieth birthday had gone by I visited the land of the dusky Ethiopians[13] and reached Memphis. There I learned things as dauntless to mortals as they are akin to infernal beings; how the Ethiopian sorcerers invoke horrid spirits, what stars, laws and affairs they long for; how they flee in fright; how they guard the gloomy Western sky and what winds oppose them; what might be the beginnings of the evil Erebos[14] and of other demons; how the souls and bodies of cattle and fish are similar; what interests the magicians and what they do; a quick course of knowledge, memory, fear, craftiness, the tracing of footsteps, a secret forgetfulness of many people, sports of people or other like things. There I learned the trembling of the earth, the origin of rain-filled clouds, and their roar, and the swelling of the earth and sea; like the truth of the eternal wisdom in an imitated form which lasts forever.

There I came to know the souls of men, both those of great strength and stature, and those of monsters and terrible giants; soul which have pressed horrid things into the gloomy air or have born alone on their back the earth as a burdened man bears a heavy weight on his shoulders. I saw the demonic conversation of the bent-backed monsters, fierce blasts which go about the earth; then there were excited devils sent forth to wander among mortals to spread myriad evils. And I saw the earth wearied by the demon, not resting upon unsteady water because of its foundation. And I was the first to see the place where adversaries are requited, a place which the serpent who tried to rival divine might hit upon for the whole twisted malicious life of humans. From it many spirits work hard at such basic things as luring humans into impious behavior. Then I learned the connection between evil and strife when it suddenly comes up against an holy person; madness against prudence; injustice against justice with no just person or even a just act present.

Then I saw the unpleasing, overly wrought form of Mendacity. It had a three form appearance of lust contriving at evil, bloodied, consumed by fire, foaming and suffused like a liver. I beheld the winged figure of Wrath, troublesome, swift, and beastly. Then I saw Deceit, continuous and secretive, attended by wily words. After that I beheld the black and blind form of Hatred from which the four eyes in its head avoided the glittering eye of radiating light. Thousands of feet, fearful only to look at, were lifted from the head to it, for it had no stomach and ferocity ate at its innerds. Jealousy and terrible Desire are similar to these others, but baneful Desire brings a tongue similar to a shovel. I saw an impudent Peevishness, like a dead body; it had many eyes and arrowed lashes -- impetuous, with its mind always occupied elsewhere. Then I viewed the form of demonic greed; it had on top, a narrow, outstretched head, two mouths, one upon its breasts and the other on its back, each feasted on the solid earth and hungered after rocky weights and flesh in abundance, digesting them by wicked-

161

ness. I saw the Avarice; it had a sharp alluring body so you were viewing a pruning hook, and its eyes were always closing with its lids. I likewise beheld Commerce, humble and swift; it bore all hope of happiness as a weight on its shoulders. I saw the form of Idleness; it had a noble soul but obese flesh; there were no white bones in it. I learned the lofty service of idols; it had two dense wings above on its head which seemed to cover it all up and nothing could be made a protection for its limbs. Then I saw the fickleness, weight, and fear of Hypocrisy; a wide chest which was really weak, riddled by secret wasting and blasted by the wind. Then I saw the form of Madness with its two natures, make and female, naked, shameless, and impotent. Then I saw a particularly reckless demon who had a tongue longer than his entire body. I beheld a fool who had a head like a filbert, a conceited soul which had done all it had ever heard of.

I learned in Ethiopia the workings of all difficult things, the form in which the shameless demons habitually go about in the universe, accursed, devilish, and monstrous; and the 365 devils of troublesome passions who had power through their conceit. I saw the great delusion of virtue, of vain wisdom and justice which deceive the wise men among the Greeks; for whoever would view an image flees the reality as shadows, and ashes are always unprofitable for everything.

In all these things the evil demons work for the errancy of many. But it is not right for me to produce unlimited books about myself; speaking about a few things among many, I have told you of my impiety. But let me mention this: that when I was thirty I left the country of the dark skinned peoples and hastened to the city of the ancient Chaldeans,[15] to learn the course of the aether which they themselves said to be of fire; these critical thinkers brought into the light what they perceived. There I learned the changing nature of the stars - as one who separates herbs from weeds - knowing the starry arrays from their opponents. They know the home and provenance of each and their allies, courts, food, drink, and the wise fellowship initiated in the light. They showed me the 365 quadrants of the silvery heavens. Such a beholder was a fellow worker with the stars, and he carried out the intentions of the heavens.

The same responsibilities were placed on the leader of the Chaldean thinkers. He developed his plan and his lonely path apart from them, concealing his plan from the hidden demons, and deriving solace only from the sacred rites. But the heavenly ones did not heed the libations, only caring for the spreading light of heaven; for I saw how he would give a share of the light to the stars and not give light to the mingled depths.

Great amazement held me captive when I saw the arbitors that cared for the dark airs of destruction. I marveled greatly indeed knowing the laws which kept them separated, according trustworthy plans. There were piety, friendship, celerity, and violent acumen: that the leader might mix them together. The leader thoroughly knew the foundations of deceit; for he was intelligent, having dragged breath from the air. Having obtained the tongue of eloquence from the fruitful earth, he learned all sorts of deceitful tricks from the inhabitants of hell. He held up the entire course of the universe persuaded that the birth of the Holy God would not take place; for he carried out all his business through beguilement, and having dispersed everything, the evil one had power on earth.

Believe me that I saw the devil himself and made many drink offerings and sacrifices to him. Believe me that seeing him and speaking to him, I heard the words of his friends. To them he addressed me as a youth, beautiful by nature, like Iambres,[16] a powerful initiate, worth of his works. Then when he saw the works of my life he promised me the leadership of the world, since I had toid for him. Honoring me, he put me into the malicious band of his evil demons, and he said to me as I left, "Cyprian, a powerful man are you."

Rising from his chair he sent me forth, and both the old and all his followers marveled. The devil appeared to be a form with gold flowers, with gleaming eyes and having on his head a wreath made of closely linked hair and gems whose brightness flooded the earth with its radiance. Similarly adorned were his clothes. Thus crowned he shook the earth while shielding some of its cities placed on the circle of its slopes. He shook trees on the earth which were like a closely arrayed military cohort, hurling lightning bolts at their feet like a god on Mt. Olympus who shines brightly on his marvels, prospering vineyards and being similarly beneficent to all for whom he is a god. Consequently he provoked strife with the immortal ruler and his saints.

Then he seems to deceive the minds of humans; he brings forth vain shadows because of which the forms of demons became visible. The unseemly group is most concerned to be seen and to obtain power on the earth. They need libations and burnt sacrifices given to them; for from the rites a great smoke rises to the heavens and dark colored shadows press down and drag on what bodies are round about, like a well-wrought cloak of fine choice wool or linen; instead of the truth they make many shadowy illusions under the high ceilinged temples enter the air. And because of an ant there is a lack of sacrificial animals and libations;[17] but water, beasts, and even fruits the devil asks for, and everything which the fruitful earth brings forth, so that he might bring delusions to mortals. In the same way we might see the forms of the dead in our mind and seem to speak to them though they are not present. In the same way the enemy removes the sacred bonds between ourselves and the dead and turns the forms of thier faces into idols so that no power is in them; rain pours down and there is no truth; a funeral pyre is like a cold ice storm. Similar it is to a man who sees a lone fish but cannot eat it or glittering gold to one who is in dire penury. But imitating the solid work he completes towns, chambers, well-wooded seashores, shady dells, flower carpets -- things which life brings about -- bearing every shadowy thing to the blood-sucking demons. In this way the night traveling demons can slumber and yet see. The demon is far ranging, like enemies and impious mortals, defiling the work of humanity.

But I suffer because having wanted to stand in awe of God, I learned of the awesome death of the chilling monster and the emptiness of his courage, and am sunk in a dark morass myself. For I know that demons were completely impotent against the holy young virgin, the venerable Justa. I saw clearly that the intelligent, scaly, huge, puffed-up, mighty, terrible monster didn't have the power of even a single mosquito.

164

I learned of the Lord through the holy virgin, after I
prayed a great deal, and did not run away from the truth.
The young woman along threw down under her feet so great a
snake. That master of far ranging idols did not dare
approach the doorstep of the awesome virgin. He urged many
spirits to attack her doors but none had power over the
young woman. He who wished to rage over the earth yielded
to a woman; he who had many cares in his heart could not over
throw her; he who ate to excess like a lion called for aid
and like a mosquito feared everything and prayed in front of
her house.

Then I left the shores of Persia, going to the great
city of Antioch in Syria. I performed many things through
the terrible techniques of magic, cures for love, malice,
hateful zeal, even evil, or whatever bothered the flesh.
Then a certain lovely Aglaides prayed as many others did,
imploring that he might be joined to his beloved, a young
woman named Justina. First a wily devil saw me; he sent out
a cohort, and they came to congregate around the holy virgin,
but were unable to get at her. The faith of the virgin
revealed Aglaides' unseen support and showed me his impo-
tence. Aglaides had many sleepless nights as I tempted
Justina through trickery and strife for seventy days and
nights until the chief demon with his own attendant cohort
came to contend against the virgin. Love alone had not
tamed young Aglaides, but desire had touched his heart.
What a marvel was the array of those devils, beseeching that
the young woman be tamed by the monster. Belial was not
beloved by us since his terrible deeds had caused us to
shudder. We told him, "If you are so powerful, have love
depart from our hearts so that we no longer suffer such
pains in vain."

And he said to the eagle, an attendant of Venus, "having
heard what I said, do what I commanded." He did many things,
but not the final work we asked. He beheld the power of the
sovereign greater through its human nature than all the
hateful demons; but when he found human nature in full bloom,
pride swelled in his great heart. Because he did not yet
see the life supporting flower of humanity, he fastened the
praise on himself for its strength, just as any weak or lame
person doing battle, seated on a horse, thinks well of his
furious rushing, and attributes great praise to himself; for
whenever love grows in adolescence it is just like a fire
catching after vigorous smoking.

165

Then a great fight broke out among the demons, who
battled each other for a long time. I addressed the monster
with hurtful words which quickly evaporated his good report
and left him mute as he beheld his evil deeds. Then he
roared and raged at everything. Finally he left quietly,
knowing he was a lesser, weaker power.

Here is what occurred when he deceived Aglaides. He led
the virgin to him, and suddenly the trick was revealed; for
Aglaides was not suitable for the arms of the holy Justina.

Then I, learning of these things, abhored the snake.
In deed I turned into a leader of people aspiring to good,
having a beauty like that of the temperate Justina. As the
demon approached Aglaides he said, "May the beauty of the
renowned Justina be golden." As he named the young girl,
the demon fled. Now the tremblings in Aglaides' breast
ended speedily.

O beloved, I myself was present at the end of these
evil affairs; I know the young woman's love for our heavenly
ruler and the cowardice of the monster. Having admitted
committing evil deeds with the evil unsleeping one, I stood
beside him, a man degraded into a woman or a flighty creature.
As I went into the house, an unseen phantom left and I
resembled again that Cyprian who had trusted in those
ancient magicians.

I saw Aglaides turned into a winged creature; coming
into the room of the young maiden, he perched on its height.
As the holy virgin cast her eyes through the clear window,
she destroyed the agile bird. The ill-fated Aglaides himself
would have fallen through the gates of death like a bird on
a pinnacle, if the beautiful and discerning maiden had not
had mercy on him, and offered a noble enticement to him so
that he would remian calmly at home, fearing God. She
quickly ordered him to withdraw from her house.

Neither sickness, pain, nor any other troublesome thing
subdued the virgin; although the evil-working demon sent
many plagues on her. Her parents grieved when the doctors
announced the end of her life. She addressed them, "O
beloved parents, for me it is not a grievous end to encounter
death. But a pain is present in my heart, not in my limbs;
just as if some sort of fiery vapor going up to heaven were
consuming my body."

Although we added many other pains to these others,
Justina put an end to the voices of the distant evil-doing
demon with the sign of the Cross. Then he harrassed her
parents with his evil deeds: killing their flocks, mules,
and cattle; but she prevailed over them, "Do not be vexed
at these matters, be glad in small things, because these are
the awesome mysteries of God."

     The terrible fate of the maiden did not escape the
neighbors' attention and they ordered a vigorous youth to
quickly marry the virgin; but she, strong in the cross of
Christ, gave spirit to her parents. Then the demon sent a
raging plague and uttered an oracle to the neighbors that
unless she gave up her ungovernable rancor and would let
herself be led to her fitting destiny, the bed of Aglaides,
the plague would continue.

     Christ's handmaid put an end to the people's outcry
for by her prayers the plague left the city. Then all who
dwelt about the city endeavored to give honor to Christ and
poured their outrage on me as the one who sought the destruction of their city. They all hated me violently. I was
ashamed, however, of both the city and the neighbors.
Seeing the very great power and deeds of the Cross, I turned
this over in my mind and spoke to the evil demon.

     "O malevolent scion of hell, giver of all lawlessness,
pity of impiety, how did you deceive my soul when you yourself knew you were both worthless and impotent? For if only
the shadow of the immortal God so easily tames you, what
will you do when He comes in person? If you tremble at the
name of Christ, how will you carry out and prosecute your
baneful works and deeds? If the throne of God wounds you so
strongly, how will you leave any trace of your own when he
is present? If his seal wards you off, how are you able to
draw off anyone from his allies on earth? Can you obtain
any cohort like the one with which he fends you off? I am
acquainted with your devious tricks, and I know your
illusions; I know you are stupid. Your gifts are ephemeral
and illusory. Your counsel is not sure, and your wisdom is
not the best. One is not true who contends against God;
they are only spectres and like mist. You destroy our
hearts and every hope, and you stir up a swarm of conflicting
cares and thoughts in our minds. You have consumed my life
with your evil, and you have destroyed with your tricks the
nature which I possessed.

How greatly have I been deceived by your intelligence!
I have been stupid and impious, having yielded in everything to you. Vainly I have studied wisdom and the books of
the ancients. Having trusted you I have been deprived of
possessions and bliss. With my parents' riches, you have
given me deprivations of spirit. If the poor and destitute
ate such things as I myself have destroyed, O lawless one,
then I might find God a little kindly disposed towards my
prayers. Alas, why have you maltreated me so? I have been
consumed, accursed one; I behold my unbreakable bonds; for
indeed I am dead although I seem to be alive, having
purchased the many furnishings of my tomb. I have driven
right through the depths of death while not yet dying. But
now it is appropriate for me to pray to God through his
glorious servants and pious luminaries, so that I might
receive mercy and compassion. Might I kiss the shadow of
the holy and most faithful Justina, that she might teach me
about the beauties of life! Flee treacherous Satan, lawless
one, terrible tyrant, you who scoff at piety and abhor
truth."

An enraged Satan rushed at me to kill me. He fought
with me, grasping me vigorously by the throat. No one was
about, nor did it seem possible to flee and evade death when
I recalled that sign of the most faithful maiden, the most
glorious Cross, in which she conquered, and I cried out,
praying, "O renowned ruler, God of the maiden, come, succor
me."

And straightway, He stretched out his hand and placed
his powerful seal on my limbs. Immediately the demon fled
like an arrow falling away or as a hurtling lance threatens.
Taking courage from the sign of Christ, I was very bold,
crying often on God himself. Then full of wrath, the
beast who wished me evil recoiled and said, "Christ, sought
by the many, does not save our allies since He abhors
impiety. He offers little to you which later he will not
utterly destroy once he has led you astray through a trick
or a wretched fate. When he leaves you behind, then you
will see what I shall do to you when you are deprived of my
power. For Christ does not receive my followers kindly.
Two things will have been destroyed then, you wretched
demon: first, the destruction of our friendship; and second,
your savior will not save you at all."

168

I listened to these words in great fear; but vainly he addressed me with such mischievous talk. Then you, blessed companions, know my groans. I speak of my iniquitous life that seeing it, you might be merciful; and tell me, if Christ is present as a solace to me, and if he hears my change of heart and aids me when I flee the terrible commands whose ways I learned."

For a while the crowd was silent; finally someone spoke to me, shrieking piercingly:

NOTES

1. Apollo: god of poetry, music and the sun.

2. Nedyporain: an unknown epithet.

3. Mithraic Phoebus: a merger of the cult of Mithras, an eastern sun god with Phoebus Apollo, the Greek-Roman god of the sun.

4. Zeus: the king of the gods.

5. Kore: another name for Persephone of Proserpina; she was seized by Pluto to be his queen in the underworld. Her grieving mother was Demeter who instituted special rites as a result of her loss.

6. Citadel of Athens: the Acropolis where, among other buildings, the Parthenon is located.

7. Mt. Olympus: the mountain upon which the gods dwell in Greece.

8. Argos: a city and region in Greece between Corinth and Sparta.

9. Tithonos: a mortal carried off by Eos, goddess of the Dawn. He was granted immortality at her request, but she forgot to ask for eternal youth so he wasted away to a voice only.

10. Artemis: virgin goddess of the hunt, moon, and child-birth.

11. Phrygia: an area in west central Turkey, south of the Sea of Marmoria.

12. Scythia: area on the north shore of the Black Sea; any northern barbarian land.

13. Ethiopia: the land south of Egypt. From the time of Homer Ethiopians were considered to be both wise and favored by the gods.

14. Erebos: son of Chaos and brother of Night; another name for the shadows of Hades.

15. Chaldea: area in southern Iraq encompassed by the Tigris and Euphrates rivers, whose inhabitants were very versed in science, astrology & alchemy.

16. Iambres: a magician, mentioned in 2 Timothy 3:8 as an opponent of Moses.

17. The context suggests that the ant is a metaphoric reference to any person inconsequential by the standards of worldly power, - in this case Justa but, also, by extension, Christ who because of Christian faith upsets the practices of paganism.

SELECTED BIBLIOGRAPHY

I. Texts and Translations

Egeria. Itineraria et Alia Geographia. Eds. E. Franceschini and R. Weber. Corpus Christianorum Latinorum, v. 175. Vienna: 1965.

Egeria. Diary of a Pilgrimage. Trans. George Gingras. Ancient Christian Writers. New York: Newman Press, 1970.

Egeria. Etheria, Journal de Voyage. Trans. Helene Petre. Sources Chretiennes. Paris: Les Editions du Cerf, 1948.

Egeria. Egeria's Travels. Trans. John Wilkinson. London: SPCK, 1971.

Eudokia, Aelia. De Martyrio S. Cypriani. Ed. A. Ludwich. Carmen Graecorum Reliquae. Leipzig: Teubner, 1897.

Perpetua. Acts of the Christian Martyrs. Ed. Tertullian. In Texts and Studies I, no. 2. Ed. J. Armitage Robinson. Cambridge: University Press, 1891.

Perpetua. The Acts of the Christian Martyrs. Trans. Herbert Musurillo. Oxford: Clarendon Press, 1972.

Proba. Cento. Ed. Carol Schenkl. In Poetae Christiani: Minores, Pars I. CSEL. Vienna: n.p., 1890.

II. Sources from Antiquity

The following works mention the authors presented in this book or comment upon the status of women in Antiquity.

Ambrose. Concerning Virgins.

Augustine of Hippo. Of Continence.
                    Of Holy Virginity.
                    Of The Good of Marriage.

173

Confessions.

Clement of Alexandria. Stromata.

Clement of Rome. Letter to the Corinthians.

Cyprian. Letter 61.
         The Lapsed.
         On the Dress of Virgins.
         Didaskalia Apostolorum

Eusebius. Ecclesiastical History.

Gregory of Nyssa.   The Life of Macrina.
                     On the Making of Man.
                     On the Soul and Resurrection.
                     On Virginity.

Ignatius. Letter to the Smyrnians.

Jerome. Letters.

Methodius of Olympus. The Symposium.

Palladius. Lausiac History.

Polycarp. Letter to the Philippians.

Socrates. Ecclesiastical History.

Sozomen. Ecclesiastical History.

Tertullian. Against Praxeas.
             An Exhortation to Chastity to his
                 Wife.

Tertullian.   On the Proscription of the Heretics.
               On Prayer.
               On Purity.
               To the Martyrs.

III. Critical Studies

       Barnes, Timothy David. Tertullian: A Historical

and Literary Study. Oxford: Clarendon Press, 1971.

Comparetti, Domenico. Virgil in the Middle Ages. Hatden: Archom Bks., 1966.

Carcopino, Joseph. Daily Life in Ancient Rome. New Haven: Yale University Press, 1940.

Clark, Elizabeth A. Jerome, Chrysostom, and Friends. New York: The Andrew Mellen Press, 1979.

Davies, J. G. "Deacons, Deaconesses, and the Minor Orders in the Patristic Period." In Journal of Ecclesiastical History, 14 (1963).

Diehl, Ernest. Inscriptiones Latinae Christianae Veterae, I. Berlin: Weidmann, 1961.

Dodds, E. R. Paganism and Christianity in an Age of Anxiety. Cambridge: University Press, 1965.

Donaldson, James. Woman: Her Position and Influence in Greece and Rome, and Among Early Christians. London: Longmans and Green and Co., 1907.

Finley, M. I. "The Silent Women of Rome." Horizon, VII (Winter, 1965).

Freud, W. H. C. Martyrdom and Persecution in the Early Church: A Study of a Conflict from the Macabees to Donatus. Oxford: Basil Blackwell, 1965.

Goodwater, Leanna. Women in Antiquity: An Annotated Bibliography. Metuchen, N. J.: The Scarecrow Press, Inc., 1975.

Grant, R. M. Gnosticism and Early Christianity. New York: Harper and Row, 1959, 1966.

Gregorovius, F. Athenais, Geschichte einer byzantinischen Kaiserin. n.p.: n.p., 1882.

Gryson, Roger. The Ministry of Women in the Early Church. Collegeville, Mn.: The Liturgical Press, 1976.

175

Histoire Mondiale de la Femme: Prehistoire et Antiquite. Ed. Pierre Grimal. Paris: Nouvelle Libraire de France, 1975.

Johnson, Mary. Roman Life. Chicago: Scott, Foresman and Co., 1957.

Jonas, Hans. The Gnostic Religion. Boston: Beacon Press, 1963.

Kelly, J. N. D. Jerome. New York: Harper and Row, 1975.

Kloeppel, Makrina. "Makrina die Jungere: eine altchristliche Frauengestalt." In Frauer in Bannerkreis Christi. Maria-Laach: Verlag ars liturgica, 1964.

de Labriolle, Pierre. The History and Literature of Christianity. New York: Barnes and Noble, Inc., 1966.

Lazzati, Giuseppe. Gli sviluppi della letteratura sui martiri nei primi quattro secoli. Torino: Societa Editrice Internazionale, 1956.

Lefkowitz, Mary R. "The Motivation for St. Perpetua's Martyrdom." In Journal of the American Academy of Religion, 44 (September, 1976).

Maintius, Maximilianus. Geschichte der christlich-latinischen Poesie. Stuttgart: n.p., 1891.

Mandelbaum, Allen. "Introduction." The Aeneid of Virgil. New York: Bantam, 1972.

Marucchi, Orazio. Christian Epigraphy. Chicago: Ares Publishers, Inc., 1974.

McKenna, Sr. Mary Lawrence. Women of the Church. New York: P. J. Kenedy, and Sons, 1967.

Morris, Joan. The Lady was a Bishop. New York: Macmillan Co., 1973.

Musurillo, Herbert. Symbolism and the Christian Imagination. Baltimore: Helicon Press, 1962.

176

Owen, E. C. _Some Authentic Acts of the Early Martyrs_. Oxford: Clarendon Press, 1927.

Poeschl, Victor. "Basic Themes." In _Virgil_. Ed. Steele Commager. Englewood Cliffs, N. J.: Prentice-Hall, Inc., 1966.

Pomeroy, Sara B. _Goddesses, Whores, Wives, and Slaves_. New York: Schocken Books, 1975.

Rahner, Karl. _On the Theology of Death_. New York: Herder and Herder, 1961.

Religion and Sexism. Ed. Rosemary Radford Reuther. New York: Simon and Schuster, 1974.

Sabbatini, T. A. "S. Cipriano nella tradizione agiographica." In _Rivista dei studi classici_, XXI (1973).

Sambursky, S. _The Physical World of the Greeks_. Trans. Merton Dagut. London: Routledge and Kegan Paul Ltd., 1963.

Schussler-Fiorenza, Elizabeth. "Feminist Theology as a Critical Theology of Liberation." In _Theological Studies_.j 36 no. 4 (December, 1975).

Shewing, W. H. _The Passion of Saints Perpetua and Felicity_. London: Sheed and Ward, 1931.

The Study of Religion in Colleges and Universities. Eds. Paul Ramsey and John F. Wilson. Princeton: University Press, 1960.

Tavard, George. _Women in Christian Tradition_. South Bend, Ind.: University of Notre Dame Press, 1973.

Trible, Phyllis. _God and the Rhetoric of Sexuality_. Philadelphia: Fortress Press, 1978.

Van der Meer, Frederich. _Augustine the Bishop_. New York: Harper and Row, 1961.

Von Aschbach, Joseph Ritter. _Die Anicier-und die Romische Dichterin Proba_. Wien: n.p., 1870.

Von Franz, Marie-Louise. "Die Passio Perpetua." In <u>C.G. Jung Aion</u>. Zurich: Roscher, 1951.

Wheelwright, Philip. <u>Metaphor and Reality</u>. Bloomington: Indiana University Press, 1962.

Wilson-Kastner, Patricia. "Macrina: Virgin and Teacher." In <u>Andrews University Seminary Studies</u>, XVII, no. 1 (1979).

<u>Women and Religion</u>. Eds. Elizabeth A. Clark and Herbert Richardson. New York: Harper and Row, Pub., 1977.

<u>Women of Spirit</u>. Eds. Rosemary Radford Ruether and Eleanor McLaughlin. New York: Simon and Schuster, 1979.

Yarborough, Anne. "Christianization in the Fourth Century: the Example of Roman Women." In <u>Church History</u> 45: 2 (June, 1976).

Zahn, Theodore. <u>Cyprian von Antioch und die deutsche Faustsage</u>. Erlangen, 1882.

Zinserling, Verena. <u>Women in Greece and Rome</u>. New York: Abner Schram, 1972.

AUTHORS

G. Ronald Kastner was born in Jefferson, New Jersey, in 1949, and grew up in Kansas City and Amenia, New York. He attended Colgate University, receiving a B.A. in Classics and French, having also studied at the University of Dijon. In 1978, after a period in Reykjavik on an American-Scandinavian Society grant and a Fulbright Fellowship, he was awarded a Ph.D. from the University of Iowa in Comparative Literature. At present he is Transportation Coordinator for the Northeast Senior Citizens' Resource Center and The Eastside Neighborhood Service, both in Northeast Minneapolis. He is active in political and human rights affairs, has delivered several papers on Byzantine literature, and supervises two dogs and two cats of classical taste.

Ann Elizabeth Millin was born in Racine, Wisconsin and grew up in St. Paul, Minnesota where she earned a B.A. in theatre from Macalester College. In 1978, she received a Master of Religious Studies from United Theological Seminary of the Twin Cities in New Brighton, Minnesota. Dr. Patricia Wilson-Kastner directed her thesis on the Cento of Proba. While at United, Ms. Millin designed and wrote a workshop on racism for local churches and has had several articles on church and race published. Currently, she is a student in the doctoral program in Theology at Vanderbilt University in Nashville, Tennessee. She teaches New Testament at Tennessee State University as well as editing and writing the nationally syndicated radio program, CONNECTION, for United Methodist Communications.

Rosemary Rader, Assistant Professor in the Department of Religious Studies at Arizona State University, is also Visiting Assistant Professor in the Department of Religious Studies at the Stanford University from January 1 - July 1, 1981. She was born in St. Leo, Minnesota in 1931, received a B.A. from the College of St. Catherine, St. Paul, Minnesota, in Latin and History; an M.A. from the University of Minnesota in Latin/Classics; and a Ph.D. in Religious Studies and Humanities from Stanford University. She has studied in Italy at Florence and Rome, as well as the Vatican School of Paleography and has received numerous fellowships and grants. She has published several reviews and articles, has completed a book manuscript on male/female friendship in early

Christian communities, and does a great deal of public speaking about related issues. She is a member of a Benedictine women's community, St. Paul's Priory, in St. Paul, Minnesota.

Jeremiah Reedy is a native of South Dakota. He attended St. John's University, Collegeville, and St. Bonaventure University before earning his bachelor's degree from the Gregorian University, Rome. He received the M.A. and Ph.D. degrees from the University of Michigan. Since 1968 Dr. Reedy has taught at Macalester College where he is currently Professor of Classics and Chairman of the Department. He is the author of Boccaccio's Poetics and co-editor of Articulating the Ineffable: Approaches to the Teaching of Humanities. Among his interests are classical linguistics, Greek philosophy and the relationship between Greek thought and Christianity.

Patricia Wilson-Kastner is presently Associate Professor of Historical and Constructive Theology at United Theological Seminary of the Twin Cities. She was born in 1944 in New York City; her family moved to Texas shortly thereafter. In 1967 she received a B.A. in English from the University of Dallas, and an M.A. from the same institution in 1969 in Theology. In 1973 she was awarded the Ph.D. from the University of Iowa. She was Visiting Assistant Professor of Historical and Constructive Theology at United Theological Seminary in New Brighton, Minnesota, from 1973-74, and returned as Assistant Professor in 1975. She has published a number of reviews, articles, and a book, Coherence in a Fragmented World (University Press of America). A priest in the Episcopal Diocese of Minnesota, she is at present in various stages of two books, one on Augustine of Hippo's theology of grace, and the other on feminism and Christology.